D0535250

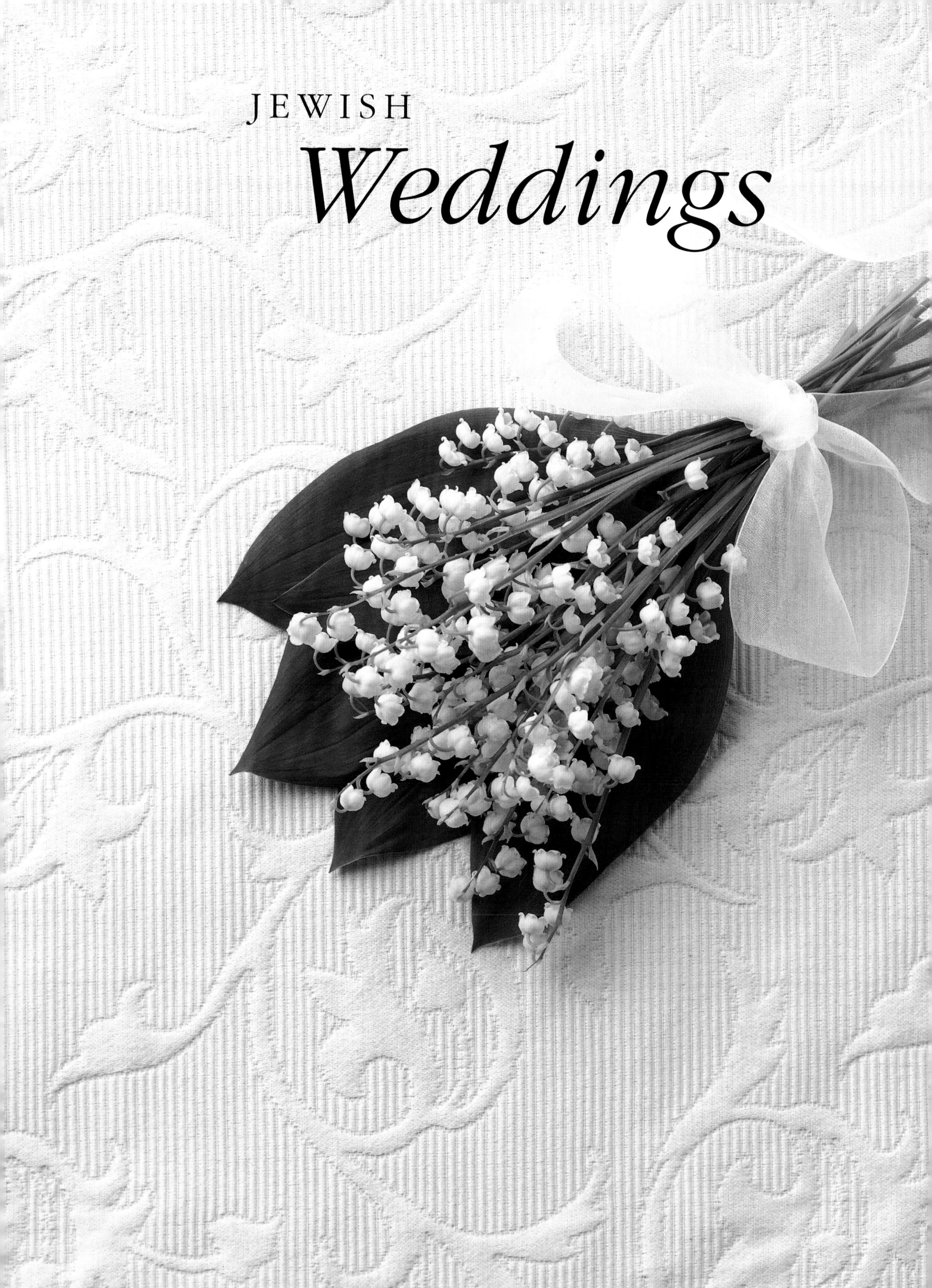

JEWISH

Weddings

קול ששון וקול שמחה
הרי את מקודשת לי
קול חתן וקול כלה
ertificate of Marriage

JEWISH *Wed*

A Beautiful Guide to Creating the Wedding of Your Dreams

RITA MILOS BROWNSTEIN

with Donna Wolf Koplowitz

SIMON & SCHUSTER

NEW YORK • LONDON • TORONTO • SYDNEY • SINGAPORE

Simon & Schuster
Rockefeller Center
1230 Avenue of the Americas
New York, NY 10020

For information regarding special discounts for bulk purchases,
please contact Simon & Schuster Special Sales at 1-800-456-6798
or business@simonandschuster.com

Designed by Rita Milos Brownstein

Manufactured in the United States of America

1 3 5 7 9 10 8 6 4 2

Library of Congress Cataloging-in-Publication Data
Brownstein, Rita Milos.
Jewish weddings : a beautiful guide to creating the
wedding of your dreams/Rita Milos Brownstein.
p. cm.
1. Marriage customs and rites, Jewish. 2. Weddings—
United States—Planning—
Handbooks, manuals, etc. I. Title.
BM713.B72 2003
296.4'44—dc21 2002075930
ISBN 0-7432-1607-5

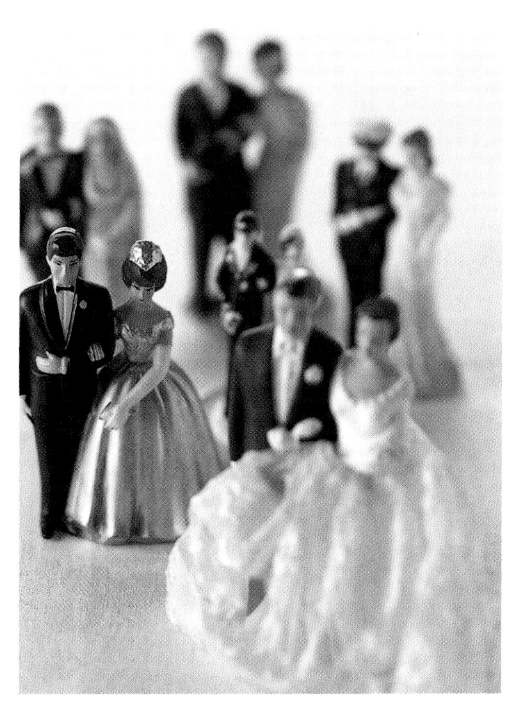

Dedicated to my husband,
Michael,
and our children,
Ariel and Ben

contents

CHAPTER FOUR

real jewish weddings 101

CHAPTER FIVE

after the wedding 147

Harmony
Delight
Protection
Love
Peace
Friendship
Mr. and Mrs.
Jay Freed
Ms. Sharon Berke
Mr. David Abrams

BEGINNING thoughts

When I married my husband, Michael, I was unaware of the wealth of beauty and ritual associated with Jewish weddings. My education ended with standing under the *chuppah* and the smashing of the wineglass.

I must admit that it is only over the last eleven years that I have begun to really discover and learn about the cultural and spiritual richness of Judaism. This journey prompted me to write my first book, *Jewish Holiday Style,* which, using style and innovation, showed how to transform the Jewish holidays into exquisite and meaningful celebrations. This beauty and meaning are nowhere more evident than in that one moment in life which is probably the most important of all—your wedding.

This book is a gift of love, dedicated to love—to all of you who have chosen your partners and have chosen to marry in the Jewish tradition. This book is my wedding gift to you, and you'll get to experience, should you choose, many of the traditions that we missed. Michael and I certainly could have used the practice of *yichud,* where the bride and groom spend a short time alone together after the ceremony and before the festivities. What a wonderful time to take a breath together, look into each other's eyes, and share a first glass of champagne as a married couple, without hundreds of pairs of eyes watching.

Make your wedding day a reflection of your love, and may it be everything that you hoped for. We wish you love, happiness, peace, and blessings for your life together.

wedding planner

❦ *Use this planner to help you organize and plan your event. You might want to copy the pages so that you write on the copies and not in the book.*

Six months to a year before

☐ Contact local newspapers to announce engagement.

☐ Select date. (See page 56 for dates that are off-limits according to Jewish law.)

☐ Choose a location for ceremony and reception.

☐ Send save-the-date cards.

☐ Choose a caterer.

☐ Plan the engagement party.

☐ Choose rabbi and/or cantor to officiate at the service. Discuss the different elements of Jewish weddings and decide what to include.

☐ Book photographer.

☐ Book videographer.

☐ Order dress and veil.

☐ Choose attendants.

☐ Choose florist or friend who will put together arrangements.

☐ Compile guest list.

☐ Book musicians for ceremony.

☐ Book band for reception.

☐ Check with your officiant about dress requirements. Does the bride need to cover her shoulders? Does the groom need to wear a *kittel* (white ceremonial robe)?

Four to six months before

☐ Reserve any rental equipment needed.

☐ Order yarmulkahs and *benchers* (prayer booklets) if needed. (Yarmulkahs may be imprinted with names and dates.)

☐ Order wedding cake.

☐ Order invitations and thank-you notes.

☐ Choose the type of *chuppah* you'd like. Check with your synagogue to see if it has one you can use.

☐ Contact the synagogue if you plan on having an *aufruf.*

☐ Purchase groom's attire.

☐ Decide on the type of *ketubah* you want.

☐ Decide on favors.

☐ Choose gifts for bridal party.

☐ Hire calligrapher, if needed.

☐ Reserve hotel rooms for out-of-town guests.

☐ If you're both of Eastern European descent, consider talking with your doctor about Tay-Sachs, a genetic disease common to Jews from that part of the world.

Two to four months before

☐ Choose menu with caterer.

☐ Purchase or make guest book.

☐ Decide on the people you'd like to hold the *chuppah,* make the blessing over challah, or read the seven wedding blessings.

☐ Decide on type of decorated bride and groom chairs.

☐ Finalize details of wedding service with rabbi and cantor.

One to two months before

☐ Have programs designed and printed. (Programs help your non-Jewish guests understand the meaning of the many Jewish traditions.)

☐ Mail invitations.

☐ Ask family and friends for an itinerary of *Sheva Brachas* dinners.

☐ Obtain marriage license.

☐ Make plans to donate wedding dress to charity, if desired.

☐ Purchase wedding bands. (Jewish law requires simple bands without precious stones.)

☐ Visit a *mikvah* (ritual bath) if you plan on incorporating this tradition into your married life.

Two to four weeks before

☐ Have final dress fitting.

☐ Decide on seating plan and write place cards.

☐ Wrap wineglass for breaking.

☐ Prepare candy for *aufruf.*

The day before

☐ Ask a friend to handle all the ritual elements—*ketubah, chuppah,* Kiddush cups, rings, and glass for breaking.

☐ Finalize seating.

☐ Start fasting at sundown to purify yourselves.

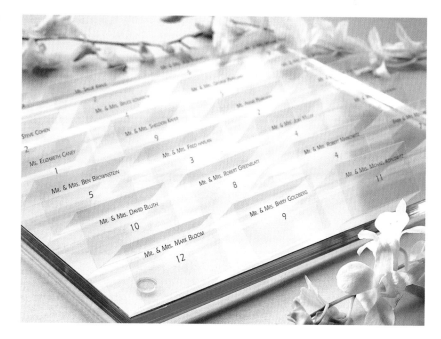

Only love
gives us the flavor
of eternity.

~Klatzkin

CHAPTER ONE

ABOUT JEWISH marriage

ACCORDING TO JEWISH TRADITION, FORTY DAYS before the conception of a baby girl, a heavenly proclamation declares exactly who the child will someday marry. Call it in vitro matchmaking, but that is how we find our *barshert*—or preordained partner.

In this chapter we'll take you on a tour of Jewish wedding celebrations and traditions throughout the ages—from biblical times, when both the bride and groom wore crowns of olive branches, myrtle, and roses, to early twentieth century weddings. You'll even get to peek in on modern-day *barshert* stories—personal stories of finding one's true soul mate.

We'll discuss the Jewish concepts of love and intimacy here and their spiritual basis. And since Judaism never gives spiritual concepts and spiritual goals without practical advice as how to achieve them, we'll also look at the concept of family purity.

In planning your wedding, you'll find it is fascinating to look back through the ages and to see where the customs and rituals came from and how the couples that preceded you celebrated, even during times of adversity and persecution.

As you celebrate your special day, you'll realize it's not yours alone: The customs and rituals are part of the unbroken chain of tradition that is the Jewish people. They are a legacy from all who came before, to be enjoyed and treasured, and are now entrusted to you, as you take your place in the 3,300-year-old chain of Jewish history.

the timeless link: a history

❦ *ABOVE: This pewter marriage plate is crafted after a painting by Moritz Oppenheim. The inscription on the rim says "Blessed art thou, O Lord, who makes the groom joyous with the bride."*

❦ *OPPOSITE: A modern-day version of the crown made by rabbinical students centuries ago, originally of olive branches, myrtle, and roses, woven with gold and silver threading.*

THE CONCEPT OF MARRIAGE IS AS old as creation itself. Thousands of years ago, at the conclusion of Yom Kippur, the young women of Jerusalem would flock to the vineyards outside the city, dressed in white robes to attract suitors.

Times have changed. Styles have changed. So have many of the old traditions. Yet they are still recognizable, and the reasons remain the same. Today, as in ancient times, the wedding ceremony consists of two parts: The first, the *kiddushin,* includes blessings, the marriage formula, and the giving of the ring. The second, the *nesuin,* includes the Seven Blessings, the breaking of the glass, and *yichud.* In ancient times these two parts took place a year apart, somewhat like today's engagement period. But as persecution increased, couples would sometimes get separated, so the rabbis decreed that both parts of the ceremony take place at the same time, which is still the custom today.

Marriage is of such central importance in Judaism that in ancient times parents would provide for their child's wedding canopy when the child was born. If the baby was a boy, they would plant a cedar tree; if the baby was a girl a cypress tree was planted. Years later the trees would be cut down and the wood combined to create the wedding litter and its canopy that covered the bride. The bride was carried on the decorated litter through the streets from her parent's home to her husband's; this was actually part of the wedding ceremony symbolizing her new status. The litter was held aloft by community men of high social status. From this procession came the modern-day custom of standing under a *chuppah.* The bride wore golden embroidered garments that emphasized her status on that day. Since it was considered a religious duty to participate in such events, young students and their rabbis would leave their studies to join in the procession.

Today, wedding gowns and tuxedos celebrate the special status of the bride and groom. In earlier times, the groom actually wore a diadem, or crown, as a sign of sovereignty (although somewhat temporary!). Rabbinical students made beautiful woven crowns for the pair, of twisted olive branches, roses, and myrtle, threaded with stones and delicate strands of gold and silver. The concept is much like the photo of the young modern-day bride on the opposite page.

For a week or two before the wedding, the couple had an escort wherever they went, and were guests of honor at many

parties and feasts. After the wedding, the groom was exempt from all army and community duties for one full year so that he could concentrate fully on giving his wife happiness. And for thirty days after the ceremony, the groom was not allowed to enter the bridal chamber without her specific permission.

A wonderful tradition born long ago still exists today: that of providing funds for poor or orphaned brides to cover the cost of a proper wedding. In European Jewish communities there were self-imposed taxes to establish and maintain such funds called *hakhnasal kallah,* kindness to the bride. Unfortunately, today there are many young women in Israel and other parts of the world in need of this assistance. Consider donating your wedding gown to an organization that handles *hakhnasal kallah*—we have some contacts in our Resource Guide. It is considered one of the greatest of all *mitzvahs* to provide such joy and peace of mind to a bride who needs financial help.

During the Middle Ages much of the Jewish population lived in small, isolated villages scattered throughout Europe as a result of the Crusades and persecution. There was little communication between villages and travel was made even more dangerous by bands of highwaymen. Filling the void was the *shadkhan,* the matchmaker. With a combination of courage and psychological acumen, he traveled between villages arranging countless marriages. The matchmaker not only had to balance hopes and dreams with needs and realities, but was expected to have enough insight to know if the marriage would be successful

❦ *OPPOSITE: Sometimes sprigs of myrtle were placed inside these large and intricate rings that often had scenes of Jerusalem on top. These rings were loaned by the community to the bride, who wore it on a ribbon or chain around her neck.*

❦ *ABOVE: The beautiful bride is Hattie Fox Bass on her wedding day in Hartford, Connecticut. The year was 1903.*

❦ *RIGHT: These rare cake toppers were used in early twentieth-century America. If you're lucky, you might find one in an antiques store.*

❦ *OPPOSITE TOP:* A ketubah *from Livorno, 1751, is depicted in classic Italian renaissance style.*

❦ *OPPOSITE BOTTOM: A watercolor* ketubah *from Persia from the marriage of Leah bat Eliahu and Yehezkiel ben Yosef, is decorated with a traditional Persian symbol—the half-moon face rising over lions. From Isfahan, 1860.*

and happy. The matchmaker not only ensured the perpetuation of the Jewish people, he was literally the glue that kept them together in troubled times as he traveled the dangerous roads bringing news and letting the isolated communities know they were not alone.

Life in the Middle Ages was so drab that a wedding was reason for the whole community to join in for a seven-day celebration that included feasting, dramatic and musical performances, jesters, and dancing. Today, at Hasidic weddings, the *mitzvah tansel*—the custom of the rabbi dancing with the bride while holding a handkerchief between them as a sign of modesty—grew out of these festive celebrations of centuries gone by. The lifting of chairs holding the bride and groom at practically every Jewish wedding today stems from this period as well.

Though large and joyous, weddings were not extravagant. Money was the usual gift, to get the new couple started properly. The wedding ring, so popular today, was, according to some authorities, introduced in the seventh century. There were also large and intricate rings owned by the community and loaned to the bride to be worn on a ribbon or a chain around her neck. Many had handcrafted gold houses on top representing the Temple in Jerusalem, and were inscribed with the words *mazel tov* for good luck. Today, of course, rings are made to be worn comfortably and every day, and the heavy rings of the past are in museums.

Another more ancient custom from biblical times is the bridal veil, which recalls our matriarch Rebecca, who covered her head with a veil as she saw her bridegroom Isaac approach.

Remember the ancient ways and how they have come to add richness and meaning to your own wedding: The processional, the dancing, the lovely meal, the *chuppah,* the veil and ring, and the one day in your life when you are truly royalty. Celebrate and practice your priceless heritage with your entire being.

Remember, also, that in addition to all the friends and family members who attend your wedding, you have an exalted guest. The Midrash says that God so greatly desires weddings that He even serves as a witness at all weddings.

Whether you choose to marry in a meadow or in a garden, in a synagogue or in a huge catering ballroom, the whispers of our ancestors are with you.

made in heaven

The 8-minute date

Enter the twenty-first century, and imagine the scene: A roomful of young Jewish singles, engaged in what looks like a huge game of musical chairs. Sitting two by two, across from each other, they have exactly eight minutes to say hello and exchange important data including careers, families, religious observance, hopes, and dreams before the buzzer rings and they wander off to their next "date," where the process is repeated again and again. Sound exhausting? It can be, but serious, marriage-minded Jewish singles have discovered a way to encapsulate the agonizing process of long evenings with blind dates into a comfortable, no-strings way of gaining introductions to other Jewish singles. Life moves quickly these days—for many singles it's often hard to meet Jewish dates. So, if this is how you met your *barshert—mazel tov*!

AS THE OLD SAYING GOES, "THERE'S someone for everyone." When you find your soul mate, your perfect partner, it's no accident, according to Judaism, it's *Barshert*.

The miracle of finding each other—on a crowded subway train, at a friend's wedding, or through a formal introduction by relatives—was not an accident, good luck, or even a smart "fix-up." The belief is that if God intends two souls to meet, He will, if necessary, bring them together from opposite ends of the world. The circumstances are orchestrated by God and the intermediaries involved are His messengers.

The last days before the wedding rush by in a blur of final details and arrangements. Everything else gradually fades into the background as family, friends, and relatives all seem to have only one focus in life. On the actual day itself the entire world is somehow transformed into a backdrop for what is about to happen. Then, in the final moments before the *chuppah,* even the heavens and earth seem to be waiting, holding their breath. And the truth is, they are. For this is a moment that has been ordained since the beginning of creation. As you stand beneath the *chuppah* you know why your heart is pounding. You see your fiancé, family, and friends, and you know your life is about to change forever. But as much as you see, there's so much more you don't. For although the *chuppah* was made on earth, the marriage was made in heaven.

Jacob and Talia may think they met because they happened to go to the same university and Jacob had a cousin who knew a friend of Talia's. But while all this may be true, it was no coincidence. For long before the hall was rented and the deposits given, even long before they first met, the greatest wedding planner of them all was hard at work. Two souls had been carefully prepared for each other, carefully fashioned and made by the Creator of the universe and then stamped *barshert,* meant for each other.

And this is why Talia and Jacob just *happened* to go to the same university, and Jacob just *happened* to have a friend who knew a cousin of Talia's. And this is why everything seems just the way it was meant to be.

Barshert Stories

Wedding Party *barshert*

Bobbi Prizant and Bob Markowitz

I met my husband at a wedding rehearsal in my hometown, Montreal. I was a bridesmaid. He was the best man and an out-of-towner. The bride, a family friend, asked me if I could do her a favor and show the best man, her fiancé's brother, our city. I was eighteen; he was an "older man" at twenty-three. My first impression was that he seemed a little conceited, but he was cute and after we exchanged some sarcastic banter, he simmered down. I'll never forget what I wore that night: it was a short-sleeved, cable-knit, melon-colored sweater and skirt. Nor will I forget that after the rehearsal, he went up to his room in the hotel and changed from a formal to a more casual outfit. After dinner I drove him around the city to see the sights. When I dropped him off at 11:00 P.M., I was charmed by his concern when he asked me to call him from home, to make sure I had arrived back safely. I did and we spoke until dawn, discussing everything from our families, to our hopes and dreams for the rest of our lives. After our soulful conversation, we were inseparable the rest of the weekend. On Sunday, following the wedding, when he kissed me good night, he asked me to marry him . . . four days after we met. When I returned home that night, I told my parents, "I think you're going to have a dentist for a son-in-law." My father said, "Just go to sleep, you're in love with a new guy every week!" (Thirty-two years later, I'm still in love and I still have the sweater.) —*Bobbi Markowitz*

Eye doctor *barshert*

Beth Friedman and Donald Salzberg

On my second date with my husband, Don, I knew we were meant to be together. We were both in our twenties, and we were married thirteen months later. This year will be our nineteenth anniversary.

One summer's night in the early 1980s I had been reluctantly cajoled by an acquaintance into attending a party he was giving. After being there a couple of hours, I was not only not having a good time, but was being annoyed by a guy who just couldn't take a hint. When he finally left me alone for a while I asked a guy who had been standing nearby if he would pretend he was with me. He said he had been standing there because he was waiting for an opportunity to talk to me.

We talked, we danced. I wasn't too interested. He asked for my number. I said I wasn't in the habit of giving it out. He said he wasn't in the habit of asking. For some reason I wrote it down, and when I was writing, he said to me, "A lefty—I'm in love." I suddenly turned around and saw him in a totally different way.

About ten years after we were married I remembered that as a teenager I used to notice a lot of people wearing eye patches and had even told a friend that someday this was going to have some meaning in my life. Then it dawned on me—the acquaintance who had given the party where I met Don was an ophthalmologist. And Don also became an ophthalmologist—a left-handed one.—*Beth Salzberg*

Soho *barshert*

Sarah Jane Freymann and Steven L. Schwartz

It was early spring, in 1975. I was living on the Upper East Side, in a beautiful apartment on the thirty-first floor, with a picture-postcard view of Manhattan. At 10:00 that particular evening, even though I was young and full of life, and my business partner David and I had been invited to a party in Soho, I had already gone to bed.

Several important changes had occurred over the past year. David and I had started our own literary agency, and by mutual consent, my engagement of six months had broken off. I was still a little heartbroken. And, paradoxically, I had also decided that I was finally ready to settle down and get married. I didn't know exactly what kind of man I was looking for, but for the first time in my life, I realized it was important he be Jewish. With all that in mind, I made what might seem like an odd decision. Some deep instinct told me that I was frittering away my energy and that if I just remained "still," the right situation would manifest itself. I decided, for a while I would give up dating altogether. That "while" turned into a year. During that time my yoga practice had deepened and had also evolved, naturally into meditation.

Which is why, on that spring evening I was perfectly satisfied to be at home—alone. I remember clearly it being 10:00 P.M. when I called my partner to tell him we had, after all, to go to that party. He said, "Sarah Jane, that's ridiculous. I'm already in bed." "I just have a feeling," I told him. There must be someone we have to meet, I rationalized, someone who would turn out to be very important to our burgeoning business. I felt a real urgency. I told David that if he didn't want to, I'd go alone. Twenty minutes later he was downstairs in a taxi.

When we arrived at the address Michael, a photographer client of ours, had given us, things seemed oddly quiet. But it was a walk-up, and who knew what, I reasoned, might be happening six floors above. Even then, in spite of the yoga, I hated climbing stairs. But up on the sixth floor, everything was dead still. Clearly, I either had the wrong address or the wrong date. Confused (and a little embarrassed), I walked back down, hoping David wouldn't be furious.

In front of the building was another couple. They, too, looked as if they had been invited to a party. I was relieved. It wasn't my mistake. I vaguely remembered having seen the woman at other "downtown" parties, and David knew her slightly, so they exchanged pleasantries. She was with a very tall, bearded man, with curly brown hair. We made eye contact, but I don't think we spoke. I told them not to bother climbing the six flights. The next day, Michael called to apologize. He had, in fact, given several people the wrong date. And that was the end of that. Or so I thought.

Several weeks later I got another, somewhat apologetic, call from Michael. Some man had called him, wanting to know about getting in touch with me. "I know who it is. It's the man from the night of the nonparty," I said before Michael could finish the sentence. "Tell him he can call me. It's fine." On our first date, as we sat eating in Steve's favorite Szechwan restaurant, he told me he had been born in the Bronx. He also told me that, after giving him a hard time and then my telephone number, Michael had said in an oddly cryptic way, "Good luck."

He and I were married nine months later and our daughter, Elisabeth, was born in July 1980. I sometimes wonder if Steve isn't still trying to figure out what Michael meant by that "Good luck." *—Sarah Jane Freymann*

Public transportation *barshert*

Rita Milos and Michael Brownstein

Having lived in New York City only one year after graduation from art school in Columbus, Ohio, I was dating young men I met through my job as a graphic designer or "fix-ups" from friends and relatives. One evening, after visiting my parents in Florida, I flew back home to New York. I was sitting alone on the express bus that goes directly from La Guardia Airport to Manhattan. A young man sat down in the seat beside me, and we started a conversation. The time flew and before we knew it, we reached our destination, Grand Central Terminal. We quickly exchanged phone numbers and agreed to keep in touch. As soon as I arrived back at my apartment, I called my mother and told her I met a nice guy on the bus and we exchanged phone numbers. She said, "Are you nuts? You gave your phone number to a perfect stranger in New York City?" "But, Mom," I answered, "he's Jewish." "Ahhh . . ." she said. That stranger turned out to be my husband of twenty-three years. *—Rita Brownstein*

Barshert Stories

The Wrong Judy

Judy Gellman and Jeffrey Pardo

Our Miami Beach *chavurah* met regularly for years. One evening we were all taking turns telling stories of how each couple met and fell in love. Soon, it was my turn.

In October 1974, I was in my sophomore year of college. I thought my birthday would go unnoticed, but in the morning, a card slipped under my door. It said, "Happy Birthday. *Love*, Judy."

Cool. A birthday card from Judy. I knew who she was. She was one of those pre-med study-holics. "Happy Birthday, Love, Judy!" I had had no idea she liked me.

That evening, some friends asked me if I wanted to share a bottle of wine. Since nothing else was going on, I said, "Sure." As I entered the room, the lights flicked on, and a crowd cheered "Happy Birthday!" I had never had a surprise party before, and I was really moved. Afterward, on the way back to my room, I asked, "Who was so nice to throw me a surprise party?" "Judy," he said. Whoa—that Judy Gellman. She must *really* like me.

I saw her a few days after that, and asked her out. Things went slowly at first, but soon, we fell in love. In the spring of our sophomore year, I asked her to marry me. We've been together ever since.

At this point in relating my treasured story, I looked at Judy with a smile, and waited for that reassuring sign of approval. Instead, Judy just looked at me with mouth agape.

"What are you talking about? I never sent you any birthday card. And, I certainly never threw you a surprise party!"

"Sure you did," I protested as I tried to save face with my friends. "I specifically asked whose room the party was in and they said—'Judy.' "

To which my Judy replied, "Judy *Epstein* That party was in Judy *Epstein*'s room, not mine."

"Oops—check please!" said my friend Charles. "Poor Judy Epstein. She buys him a card, she throws him a party, and he goes out with someone else."

Well, my Judy and I will have been married for twenty-three years, and we have four wonderful children. —*Jeffrey Pardo*

On the Boat to America

Margit Yosowitz and Howard Milos

The year was 1947. World War II was over, and I was alone, since my parents, sister, and brother were all killed in concentration camps. Although I planned on going to Israel to make a new home for myself, my aunt and uncle in Cleveland urged me to join them and come to the United States. The trip by ship from Sweden to New York took one week. On the boat, at the assigned dinner table was a young German-Jewish man named Hans (Howard). Since he spoke only German and I spoke Yiddish, we really could not communicate very well, but he tried to speak with me at every meal and took pictures of me and my companions on the ship. (In fact, he followed me all around the ship!) When we reached New York, I gave him my aunt's address so that he could send me the photos he took.

Unfortunately, I did not stay in Cleveland very long. I had contracted tuberculosis while in concentration camp and had to go to a hospital in Denver. Meanwhile, Howard sent me the photos he took of me on the boat. I sent him a thank-you note and of course my return address was Denver. Since he was planning on moving to California, he hopped off the Greyhound bus in Denver, and walked into the hospital on visiting day. When the nurse told me "Someone is here to see you," I couldn't imagine who it was. After all, my family was all gone and I didn't know a soul in Denver. When Howard walked into the room, I was stunned. He stayed until visiting hours were over (by now we both learned how to speak English) got a job in Denver, and came every Sunday to visit me for the next three years, until I was released from the hospital.

When I was finally released, we drove to Cleveland and got married at the home of my uncle and aunt. We planned on moving to California, but never made it. We settled in Cleveland, raised two daughters, and spent twenty-five years there until we moved to Florida in 1975. —*Margit Milos*

love and intimacy

A Bride's Prayer

May it be thy will that Thy presence dwell between my husband and me . . . give to my husband and to me purity of soul, that neither of us fix our gaze upon any other and I regard only him, and he, only me. May he be in my eyes as if there were no other man in the world, and may I be in his eyes as if there were no other woman in the world. . . . May it be Thy will that our marriage prosper in accordance with the laws of Moses and Israel. A marriage in which there will never be anger or bitterness, jealousy or envy, but only fraternity, peace, patience, love, and kindliness. . . . As I prepare for immersion . . . purify us with Thy holiness and bless us with the blessings of heaven above all the days of our life.

MARRIAGE, LOVE, AND INTIMACY ARE gifts from God. For just as God created our physical world, He also created the institution of marriage, the emotion of love, and the pleasures of intimacy. It may be hard to imagine in our contemporary society, but throughout most of history marriage was often merely a way for a man to acquire another piece of property. And sex was considered either a necessary sin or for the benefit of the man only, without any thought or consideration given to the woman.

But three thousand years before the sexual revolution, self-help books, and marriage therapists of today, love and intimacy already existed in a form so exalted that even our modern era still hasn't caught up. For within Jewish marriage, sex and intimacy are both natural and holy. The Torah actually requires a Jewish man to be sensitive to the sexual fulfillment of his wife, and this is symbolic of his obligation to be attentive to all his wife's needs. It is interesting to note that over one-sixth of the Talmud is devoted to women's issues and rights.

Much has changed in three thousand years. It is safe to say that today, few brides would be thrilled to see a donkey among the wedding gifts. However, there is one gift that has been available to every Jewish couple. It is a guide to ensuring the success of the marriage and to achieving the greatest happiness. It is called "family purity."

The practice of family purity revolves around the woman. It places her at the center and is based on the ebb and flow of her inner rhythms and cycles. Essentially, it means that for approximately twelve days following the onset of her menses, the couple refrains from all physical contact. This includes not only sexual relations but even incidental contact like touching hands.

To those unfamiliar with family purity, the imposition of such blanket rules on the most intimate and personal part of a relationship may seem repressive and harmful. But those who practice family purity invariably report just the opposite: Just as dating, the wedding, and the honeymoon were all special times, so family purity is a way of making this important part of life more special and exciting—always. The sages state that part of the reason for the physical separation each month is to make the couple more beloved and desirous of each other.

Before the couple may resume relations, the woman must immerse herself in the waters of a Jewish ritual bath called a *mikvah*. There is a misconception that this is because the woman is considered to be made physically "impure" by her menstruation. Although this is true for many other cultures, it is absolutely *not* the case in Judaism—as evidenced by the fact that an unmarried woman does not have to do the same after her menses. Jewish men and women each for their own separate reasons, have always sought the spiritual blessings bestowed by the waters of the *mikvah*.

Today, many traditional men go to the the *mikvah* before Shabbat each week. Male and female converts also undergo *mikvah* as part of the conversion process.

The alternating periods of intimacy and separation each month provide a balance and harmony to the relationship. Although important every day, friendship, respect, and understanding are deepened and refined during separation.

As the end of separation draws near, there is a growing sense of anticipation. It may fall on a routine workday like any other, but for the couple, it is the most special day of the month. That night the husband will await his wife's return from the *mikvah*. Although many years may have passed, she will say the bride's prayer and immerse in the waters of the *mikvah* just as she did for the first time—the day before her wedding. And, if the couple feels some of the happiness and excitement of that day, or even a bit like newlyweds on a honeymoon, it makes perfect sense. Because this is God's plan and gift, delivered monthly by the waters of the *mikvah*.

Mikvah 101

A *mikvah* is any body of "living water," *mayim hayyim*. Ponds, lakes, and rivers are natural *mikvahs*. Indoor *mikvahs* are more like small swimming pools and must be connected to a natural source of water like a stream or collected rainwater. All natural sources of water are considered connected to the water that flows out from the Garden of Eden and in that sense are considered pure and pristine. In Jewish communities, the establishment of a *mikvah* is even more important than that of a synagogue and takes priority over it.

The first time a woman is obliged to immerse in the *mikvah* is the night prior to her wedding; therefore, every effort should be made to plan the wedding during that period of the month when it is permissible for the couple to have marital relations. Among some Jewish circles it is customary for the groom to also immerse in the *mikvah*. While doing so, he should silently confess his sins and resolve not to repeat them. Men and women are never at the *mikvah* at the same time. Men go in the daytime while woman go after nightfall.

Sephardic Jews have a custom of celebrating when the bride or groom returns from the *mikvah*. You may want to celebrate with this tradition after your return from the *mikvah*. It may be as simple as some wine and cheese with some of your closest friends in the lobby of the *mikvah*.

Every *mikvah* has an attendant, or "*mikvah* lady" as she is often called, to assist you. Not only will she check you before immersion to be sure you have followed all the rules (no nail polish, jewelry, bandages, etc.), but she will help you with the prayers said just prior to immersion. Most *mikvah*s have fluffy towels and nice terry cloth bathrobes and hair dryers, but you may want to bring your own, as well as your own toothbrush, shampoo, and deodorant. You will need to soak in a tub for at least twenty minutes before taking a shower. This step may be done at home, or in the *mikvah*'s tub. (If it is not a busy night, soak as long as you like with some bubble bath and a good book!) After soaking, you will shower, shampoo, and comb your hair. You are now ready to call the *mikvah* lady by ringing a bell for her. You will dunk under water a total of three times; then you return to the bathroom to dress. There is usually a small fee for the use of the *mikvah,* depending on where you live.

*Love makes
two of one
and
one of two.*

~Abravanel

CHAPTER TWO

BEFORE THE wedding

Admit it. Announcing your engagement is truly one of life's most exciting moments, and the time before the wedding one of life's busiest. The decisions, details, and planning that must be worked out turns every couple into instant CEOs with their parents serving as the board of directors.

From color planning to invitations, flowers to food, it all adds up to the usual agony and ecstasy common to all weddings. Tension is at an all-time high, especially with too many managers, but planning a wedding is still a labor of love. To ease your way, we share a wealth of beautiful ideas for you to consider when planning a Jewish wedding. Choose some, pass on others—use this book as a springboard for ideas.

We show you magnificent *ketubahs,* or wedding contracts, to make your pledges to each other even more beautiful, and create a lasting piece of artwork for your home. Bridal showers with creative and meaningful Jewish twists. A bit of education, too, introducing you to some beautiful customs you may have not considered—like the *aufruf,* a special ceremony that creates lifelong happy memories.

Our wish is that you discover, within these pages, the keys that will make your wedding even more special than you could have wished for, with all the touches that will be yours alone. An old Jewish expression goes something like this: "The way something begins is the way it will go." And we believe it. We offer you a chapter of great beginnings.

the engagement party

❦ *OPPOSITE: The plate is smashed by both mothers-in-law, to symbolize the breaks in their relationships with their children. The mothers retain a piece for themselves for good luck and distribute the broken pieces to unmarried women as a wish that they may have a joyous wedding.*

WHILE THE PROPOSAL IS USUALLY A private matter, celebrating the engagement is not. There are aunts and uncles, sisters and brothers, cousins and friends, and let's not forget the in-laws—all of whom want to celebrate and get to know one another. So if you're a little anxious, it's inevitable. The best way to get everyone in your new extended family off to a good start is with a wonderful engagement party.

Engagement parties are hardly new in Jewish tradition. One thousand years ago it was customary to have a formal party to announce the couple's engagement to the community. It was called the *tenaim,* meaning "conditions," and it was a formal ceremony where a contract was signed outlining certain prenuptial conditions between the parents. Specified were the date and place of the wedding, how the expenses were to be covered, and any gifts to the couple to get them started off in life. At the end of the *tenaim* ceremony, it was customary for the two mothers to wrap a plate in cloth and, together, break it over a table corner or chair.

Today, although many people continue to enjoy engagement parties, few have them with *tenaim* ceremonies. This is because if any of the prenuptial agreements are not carried out as promised, because of a sudden change in financial status, for example, it causes complex problems from the point of view of Jewish law. For this reason, in those Jewish circles that still have *tenaim* ceremonies, they are done moments before the actual wedding, so there is no chance of the promises not being kept.

Although we don't advise having a *tenaim* party, we do advise giving your engagement party a decidedly Jewish twist. Toasts of *"L' Chaim"* (To life) together with a few words of advice from your rabbi or sage friend are a good combination of spirituality and festivity. Give the two mothers a chance to take center stage by retaining the custom of breaking of the plate. The shards are distributed among the bride's unmarried friends for good luck in finding their *barsherts.* Often, the pieces are crafted into costume jewelry before they are distributed.

Yes, it's your party—one of the first of your special days. And for many couples the excitement in the air is not made any less by the fact that the future in-laws may be meeting for the very first time.

There is no better way to ensure that the coming together of the two families starts on as warm a note as possible than to make certain the occasion is accompanied by a wonderful meal.

Our menu offers your guests a meal that not only looks elegant and tastes delicious but is simple to prepare. Since the soup and chicken breasts can be prepared a day in advance, unhurried time can be enjoyed with friends and family members who have gathered together to celebrate the beginning of your new life.

Our menu works for six guests or for thirty-six. (We've done it for fifty-six, but who's counting?) The results are a rewarding, velvety pareve cream soup. Pastry-wrapped chicken breast with a savory surprise inside. A blend of rices. And the simplicity and grace of poached pears that make traditional sweet desserts seem excessive and overdressed.

For a fabulous beginning, serve creamy, rich potato leek soup that doesn't contain a drop of cream. The potatoes do an admirable job of thickening the broth, and plump, fresh, flavorful leeks are available all year at your greengrocer. Make the soup ahead a day or two, and simply heat it on the day of the party. Float a tiny tied bundle of matchstick-sized chives on the soup for a special garnish.

For the chicken, all you need is a bit of organization and a couple of friends. First, sauté the vegetables for the filling. Add spices, bind the filling with bread crumbs, and set it aside. Pound the chicken breast flat, and cut it in half. Thaw your frozen pastry shells—they come six to a box. Dust a board with flour, roll the pastry thin, and you're ready to go. Scoop a generous tablespoon of filling onto the chicken breast, and transfer the breast onto the thin pastry. Pull the two sides together, and then close up with the opposite corners, so you end up with a neat package. Place the package, seam-side down, on a baking pan, and brush it with beaten egg.

On the morning of the party, tie your green bean bundles with natural raffia, available by the hank at craft shops. Then, just dunk the bundles into the steamer, and serve hot or at room temperature, perhaps with a tangy vinaigrette.

Add some sinful luxury to your poached pears with a silky bath of dark chocolate. It takes just a minute: melt pareve chocolate chips with a teaspoon of margarine in a small pan, whisk, and pour gently over the pear stems.

Your party will be a triumph, making everyone look forward even more to the wonderful events to come.

❦ OPPOSITE: Serve our elegant, simple-to-prepare entree of chicken breasts wrapped in pastry. Green beans and a blend of rices make the perfect accompaniments.

Engagement Party Menu

Potato and Leek Soup

Chicken Breasts in Pastry with Mushroom Sauce

Green Bean Bundles

Blend of Wild and White Rice

Poached pears

Luxe add-ons

Tie your steamed or roasted green greens into neat bundles, using a strip of red pepper or craft store raffia. If you're using the raffia, buy natural only and soak it for a few minutes first to make it pliable and easy to tie. Gather a healthy bundle of steamed (al dente) beans, loop with the raffia, and tie in a bow.

Want to give your pastry-wrapped stuffed chicken an exotic taste? Add two teaspoons of a good curry powder to your stuffing mix, and a bit for the gravy. Buy an aromatic, rather than spicy, rice blend.

Add the heaven of chocolate to your poached pears for dessert—it's easy. Melt some dark pareve chocolate chips in a small saucepan with a tablespoon of margarine or shortening (to give it a silky gloss). Then dribble over the pears—from the stem down. It looks like a still life painting, and satisfies the chocolate lovers in the group.

CHICKEN BREASTS IN PASTRY WITH MUSHROOM SAUCE

SERVES 6

1 (10-package) frozen puff pastry shells, thawed
3 boneless chicken breasts
Salt and pepper to taste

FILLING

2 tablespoons olive oil
1 onion, chopped
2 teaspoons chopped garlic
2 zucchinis, cleaned and chopped
⅓ cup chopped walnuts
3 tablespoons bread crumbs
Salt and pepper to taste
1 egg, beaten

MUSHROOM SAUCE

2 tablespoons margarine
1 tablespoon chopped parsley
1 teaspoons chopped garlic
1 small onion, chopped
1 tablespoon flour
1 cup beef broth
1 cup thinly sliced mushrooms
¼ cup white wine

1. Thaw pastry shells in refrigerator.
2. Pound chicken breasts to flatten slightly. Sprinkle with salt and pepper and set aside.
3. *To prepare filling:* In a medium sauté pan, heat olive oil. Over medium heat, add the chopped onion and garlic. Cook about 10 minutes. Add zucchini and cook for another 10 minutes. Remove from heat and stir in the chopped walnuts, bread crumbs, salt and pepper. Let the filling cool slightly.
4. On floured surface, roll out pastry shells into circles about 8 inches in diameter. Put half a chicken breast in the center of one of the circles, and put ¼ to ⅓ cup of the sautéed vegetables on top. Roll chicken breast up, bringing edges up, and place seam-side down. Repeat with remaining chicken breasts. Refrigerate. (Can be prepared a day ahead at this point.)
5. Preheat oven to 350°F. Brush tops of chicken packets with beaten egg. Bake on a greased baking pan uncovered for 45 minutes, until golden brown. If dough starts to get too brown, cover loosely with foil.

To prepare sauce:

1. In a small pan, heat 1 tablespoon of the margarine. Add the parsley, garlic, and onions, and cook over medium heat about 4 minutes. Stir in the flour. Slowly add the broth, stirring constantly.
2. In a skillet heat the remaining margarine, add the mushrooms, and sauté 5 minutes. Combine with the sauce and simmer 15 minutes. Add the wine and bring to a boil. Keep warm until ready to serve.

Presentation:

Place stuffed breast on center of plate. Spoon sauce around the packet. Garnish with parsley. Serve with wild rice and green beans.

POTATO AND LEEK SOUP

SERVES 6

3 cups leeks, cleaned and sliced
3 cups peeled, diced potatoes
5 cups chicken broth
Salt and pepper to taste
Chopped chive for garnish

1. Place the leeks, potatoes and chicken broth in a large pot and bring to a boil over high heat. Lower the heat and simmer, partially covered for 30 minutes, or until vegetables are tender.
2. In a food processor fitted with a steel blade, process soup in batches.
3. Pour back into pot, and add salt and pepper to taste. Garnish with the chives before serving.

POACHED PEARS

SERVES 6

1 bottle Merlot
1 star anise
3 whole cloves
Zest of one orange
¼ cup sugar
6 Bosc pears, peeled with stem left on

1. Combine wine, spices, zest, and sugar in a nonreactive saucepan. Bring to a boil, reduce heat, and simmer 5 minutes.
2. Add the pears, stem ends up, and cook uncovered about 30 minutes or until pears are tender. Spoon liquid over pears occasionally.
3. Remove pears to a bowl. Bring poaching liquid to a rapid boil and reduce by half. Pour the syrup over the pears and refrigerate covered for at least 5 hours.

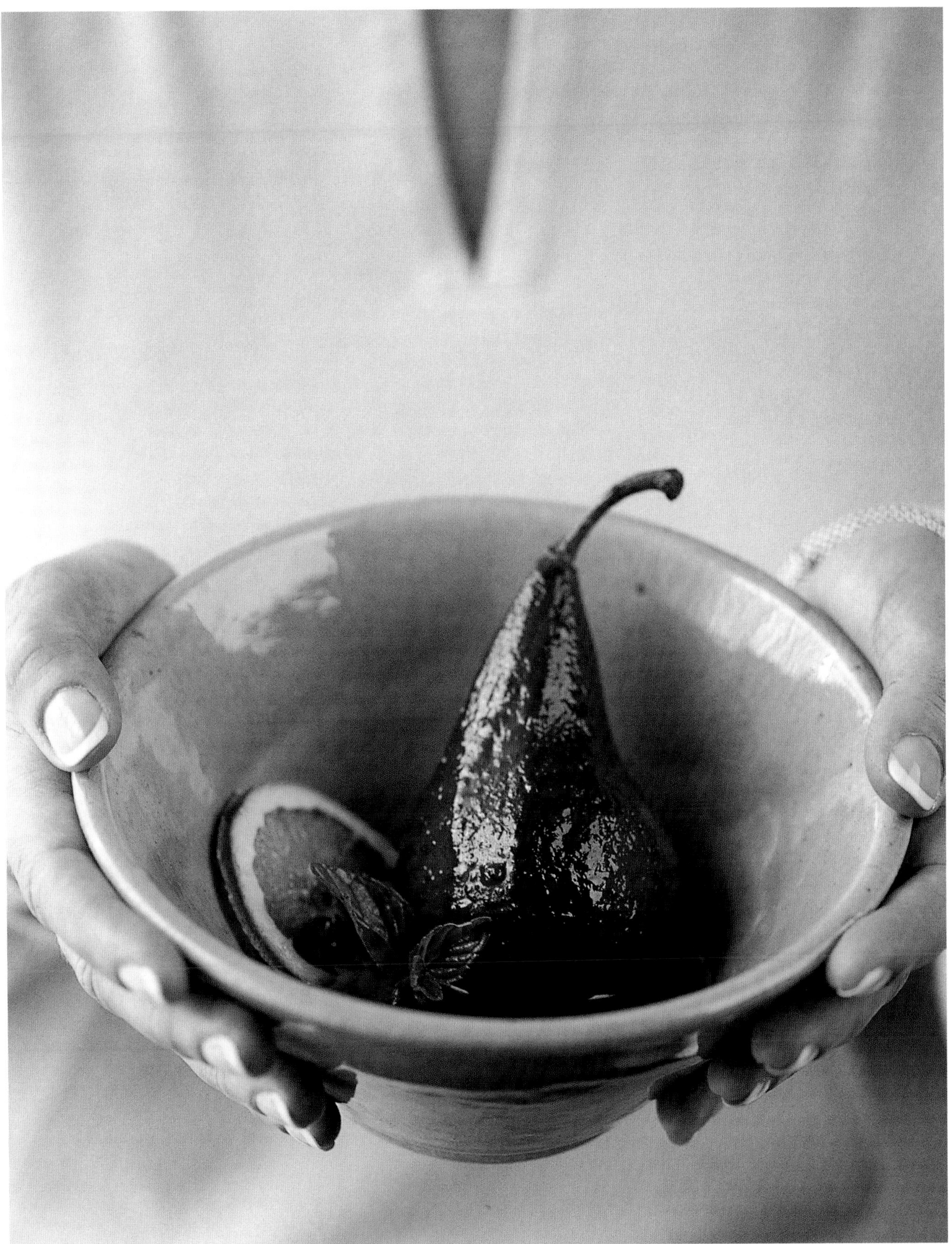

❦ *Poached pears make an elegant presentation.*

the jewish bridal shower

❦ *ABOVE: Guests write their "assigned quote" on a tag to help explain the reason behind the gift.*

THE JEWISH BRIDAL SHOWER—a perfect theme for a bridal shower that's fun and entertaining. This party is a natural and the Torah is the perfect gift registry. Here's what to do: Write a commandment or Jewish saying on each invitation, and send the invitations off to the guests.

"Remember the Shabbat day and keep it holy" lends itself to wonderful, much appreciated shower gifts, including Sabbath candlesticks or a lovely monogrammed Kiddush cup. A bread machine with a treasured challah recipe tucked inside is also a thoughtful offering.

Try another: "There can be no joy without food and drink." Some gift ideas are a state-of-the-art juicer, a food processor, or a set of cookware.

Each guest should attach the quote or saying to the gift box along with the gift tag.

We've given you lots of suggestions on the following pages that you can easily personalize for each invitation with your computer. To find more, try your local Judaica store or synagogue bookshop. There are also many anthologies available, some listed in our References section, on Jewish proverbs and sayings that are easily ordered over the Internet.

The invitations for this shower (pictured opposite) were created on the computer on a thick, touch-me vellum from an art supply store (what would we do without these stores full of wonderful ideas just waiting to happen?). Punch a couple of holes at the top, center on a heavier paper, and tie with wired ribbon, available in a dream palette of colors, textures, and weaves. A reminder: When setting up your invitation size, make sure you find compatibly sized envelopes.

Although a bridal shower can take place any time, with any kind of meal, we like the idea of an afternoon tea, just for ladies. It's a no-rush, luxurious, and laid-back time off for everyone, and a happy, stress-free time for the bride-to-be. Take pictures and videos and make it memorable. If you do decide to include the men, consider a heartier meal.

Whether you're already an *aishes chayil* (woman of valor) or a work in progress, you already know that doing everything with just that bit of extra effort pays off.

Take flowers, for instance. There may be a snowman in your front yard, but you can grow spring bulbs on a windowsill in time for your tea. Visit your neighborhood garden center for a sack of paperwhite or hyacinth bulbs, a bag of gardeners' gravel, and a two-minute lesson at the nursery desk.

You're invited to a
Jewish Bridal Shower for
Ali Kamenetsky

Sunday,
February 11, 2001
1:00–3:30 pm
32 South Woodland St.
Englewood, New Jersey
Each guest has been given a different quote
with a Jewish theme. Yours is:
"There can be no joy without food and drink"
—The Talmud
Gift ideas: cookware, china, flatware,
small kitchen appliances
Please include the quote on your gift

❦ *CLOCKWISE FROM TOP: Sweets, pretty sandwiches, special dishes, and lots of love from favorite friends make this kallah's shower memorable; bride-to-be Ali and a friend smile for the camera at her special tea; the advice book offers sage advice from friends—a keepsake for future contemplation; quotes are tagged onto gifts to make each offering even more meaningful.*

For our tea we used a separate buffet table, loaded with choices: different sugars, lovely spoons and napkins, and loads of delicious tea choices. We like the attractive wooden Wissotsky tea box from Israel that opens to reveal at least eight different kinds of teas to try.

We used cookie cutters to transform ordinary sandwiches into elegant offerings. Garnishes on the platters, such as fresh herbs and slivers of orange peel, give a fragrant scent to the table. The flavored butters used in the curried egg salad sandwiches and the salmon and cucumber sandwiches give them a wonderful flavor.

In place of one large cake, we substituted cupcakes—just for fun, stacked on two plate stands. Our petits fours are personalized with the initials of the bride and groom to be. These can be purchased from a local bakery.

Pass around an "advice book" for the bride-to-be to take home as a special keepsake. Each friend writes some sage advice for married life while a designated photographer takes candids of the advice-givers for each page. A purchased journal is fine—just create a label with your printer, or hand-letter with a slant-nib calligraphy marker.

Putting your handiwork, creativity, and love into this shower makes it a special event—one that may make the couple a little more aware of their Jewish heritage as they use the gifts they received on a day that will remain memorable over the years.

Some Ideas for Invitation Themes

"Remember the Shabbat day and keep it holy"—EXODUS 20.8
Gift ideas: Shabbat candlesticks,
Havdalah set, challah board and knife, Kiddush cup

"Man does not live by bread alone"—DEUTERONOMY 8.3
Gift ideas: A crock pot, a KitchenAid mixer, serving dishes.

"You shall not wear combined fibers—
wool and linen together."—LEVITICUS 18.19
Gift ideas: Matching his and hers cotton terry bathrobes.

"Charity lengthens one's days and years"—TANA DEVE'
Gift ideas: A beautiful *tzedakah* box

"There can be no joy without food and drink"—TALMUD
Gift ideas: A state-of-the-art juicer, a food processor, or a set of cookware.

"Honey and sweets brighten the eyes of man"—TALMUD, YOMA
Gift ideas: Basket filled to the brim with baking supplies

"Everyone is a king in their own home"—AVOT DE RABBI NATHAN
Gift ideas: Beautiful bed linens, luxurious towels

"As you shall write them upon the doorposts of
your house and your gates"—DEVARIM 6.5, 9
Gift ideas: Mezuzah including a beautiful case

"The body is the instrument of the soul, to carry
out all its works. "—RAMBAM
Gift ideas: Shower massage, foot massage, spa in a box,
luxurious feather mattress pad

"A time to plant and a time to sow "—ECCLESIASTES 3,2
Gift ideas: Gardening supplies, perennials,
beautiful garden statuary, mini trees for Tu B'Shevat

"Who studies gladly for a single hour will learn vastly more than one
who studies glumly for hours on end "—HAYYIM OF VALOZHIN
Gift ideas: Books or CD on the subjects that are of interest to the
bride and groom, a set of books of Jewish study—mysticism or
Kabbalah, is very popular right now

We've done a dairy meal here for tea, but use your imagination to create meat fillings for our sandwiches, too. Just remember to serve a pareve dessert when serving meat.

The special touches mean so much. Since this is most likely a ladies-only afternoon, enjoy the comradeship of women. Serve sherry or a sweet cherry Kijafa in delicate glasses. Live music is special, too. Talk a cello-playing friend or a brother who plays jazz piano into being your mood music—remind them that they're doing it for love!

Don't forget sweet tea breads—easy to make and always moist and wonderful when served with flavored butters or cream cheese. Save cans of all sizes and bake your sweet breads in various rounds. And flavors? Try pumpkin, zucchini, date nut, banana, lemon poppy, coconut orange, and apricot pecan. They freeze well, so make them ahead of time.

CREAM CHEESE AND ORANGE HONEY SANDWICHES

MAKES 10 SANDWICHES

Orange honey can be found in the honey section at your supermarket.

2 (8-ounce) packages cream cheese
1¼ cups walnuts
2 tablespoons half and half
Kosher salt and fresh ground pepper to taste
20 slices cinnamon bread
Orange honey spread

1. In a food processor fitted with a steel "S" blade, process cream cheese, walnuts, and half and half until smooth. Season to taste with salt and pepper.
2. Remove crusts from bread. Spread orange honey spread on one slice. Spread cream cheese filling on other slice. Form a sandwich with the two halves. Slice in half to form a rectangle.

SALMON AND CUCUMBER SANDWICHES

MAKES 10 SANDWICHES

Using a heart-shaped cookie cutter will make these sandwiches especially pretty.

2 (7½ ounce) cans of salmon, flaked and mashed
Mayonnaise to taste
20 slices potato or country white bread

MINT BUTTER

1 cup butter, softened
½ cup fresh mint
1 teaspoon lemon juice
½ teaspoon salt and pepper
1 cucumber sliced

1. In a large bowl, combine salmon with the mayonnaise.
2. *To make the mint butter:* Combine butter with mint, lemon juice and salt and pepper, in the bowl of a food processor.
3. Using a heart shaped cookie cutter, cut bread into hearts. Butter one half with the mint butter and the other half with the salmon mixture.
4. Add a slice or two of cucumber before assembling the sandwich. Serve immediately.

CURRIED EGG SALAD SANDWICHES

MAKES 10 SANDWICHES

6 hard-boiled eggs
Mayonnaise to taste
1 tablespoon curry powder
Salt and pepper to taste

WATERCRESS BUTTER

1 cup butter, softened
½ cup fresh watercress
1 teaspoon sugar
1 teaspoon salt
20 slices soft pumpernickel bread

1. In a food processor fitted with a steel "S" blade, process eggs until just finely chopped. Add mayonnaise, curry, and salt and pepper.
2. *To make the watercress butter:* Combine butter with watercress, sugar, and salt in the bowl of a food processor.
3. Using a round cookie cutter or a glass, cut bread into circles. Butter one piece with the watercress butter, and the other with the egg salad.

RUSSIAN TEA COOKIES

MAKES 30 COOKIES

Prepare the dough several weeks in advance and refrigerate until ready to bake.

½ cup unsalted butter
½ cup vegetable shortening
⅓ cup granulated sugar
2 teaspoons vanilla
2 cups flour
1 cup chopped walnuts
Powdered sugar for coating

1. Preheat oven to 375°F.
2. Cream together butter, shortening, and sugar. Add vanilla, flour, and walnuts, and beat until mixture comes together. If it is too dry, add a teaspoon or so of water.
3. Cover the dough and refrigerate at least 3 to 4 hours (The dough will keep for several weeks in an airtight container in the refrigerator.)
4. Scoop the dough with a 1-ounce ice cream scoop, or drop by teaspoons and roll into balls, flattening slightly on the bottom.
5. Bake on an ungreased cookie sheet for 10 to 15 minutes. Let cool 10 minutes on the cookie sheet and then roll in powdered sugar. Set on a rack to cool completely.

❦ *CLOCKWISE FROM TOP LEFT: Basic white-iced cupcakes borrow some "wow" from the delicate edible sugared pansies; Ali discovering her gifts; tea table; good friends; simple double-wick Havdallah candles make pretty party favors; Russian wedding cookies heaped high above petits fours.*

the *aufruf*

WITH THE SPOTLIGHT MOSTLY ON the bride during the weeks before the wedding, the *aufruf* is a celebration traditionally just for the groom. *Aufruf* literally means "the calling up," when the bridegroom is called up to read the Torah in the synagogue. This symbolic act represents his continued commitment to Torah as a married, or completed, man.

In fact, the *aufruf* can best be described by the bystander as a Shabbat morning service that combines the solemnity of the upcoming marriage with the abandonment of a full-fledged food fight!

During the service the groom is called up to say a blessing over the Torah, and as he finishes, he is literally pelted from all sides with nuts and soft candies, thrown by the congregants. As the entire congregation sings the *"Mazel tov, siman tov"* song, young children scramble in droves to collect the goodies around the *bimah*. Mothers always shake out small pockets carefully on laundry day after an *aufruf*! It is complete chaos, yet utterly joyful.

Some history on the *aufruf:* It is said that King Solomon encouraged acts of kindness among Jews, and so he constructed two gates to the Temple—one for mourners and one for bridegrooms. Fellow Jews would sit outside the gate and extend their warm wishes as the bridegrooms entered the Temple, as a sign of caring and love. When the Temple was destroyed, the rabbis continued to honor bridegrooms by inviting them into their synagogues to be honored before

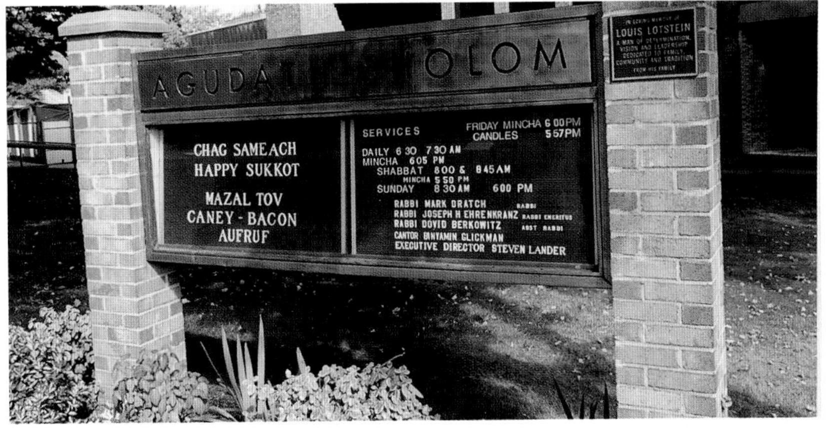

their weddings. Women in the community would throw nuts at the groom to ensure a fruitful union, and sweets to allude to the sweetness of love and married life.

After services, the groom's parents customarily host a festive *kiddush* for members of the congregation and invited guests, to honor the bridegroom. The *aufruf* takes place on the Shabbat before the wedding and is truly a *simcha*, or festive affair. Since most of the attention is generally focused on the bride, the *aufruf* makes the *chazen* (groom) feel special.

This beautiful morning is sure to become a lifetime memory.

❦ *OPPOSITE: It is a tradition to throw candy and nuts at the groom after he completes his aliyah. Prepare these bags a day in advance. The candy signifies the wish that the couple have a sweet life and the nuts are a fertility blessing.*

❦ *ABOVE: A synagogue announces a joyous event, an* aufruf, *open to all members of the congregation.*

the *ketubah*

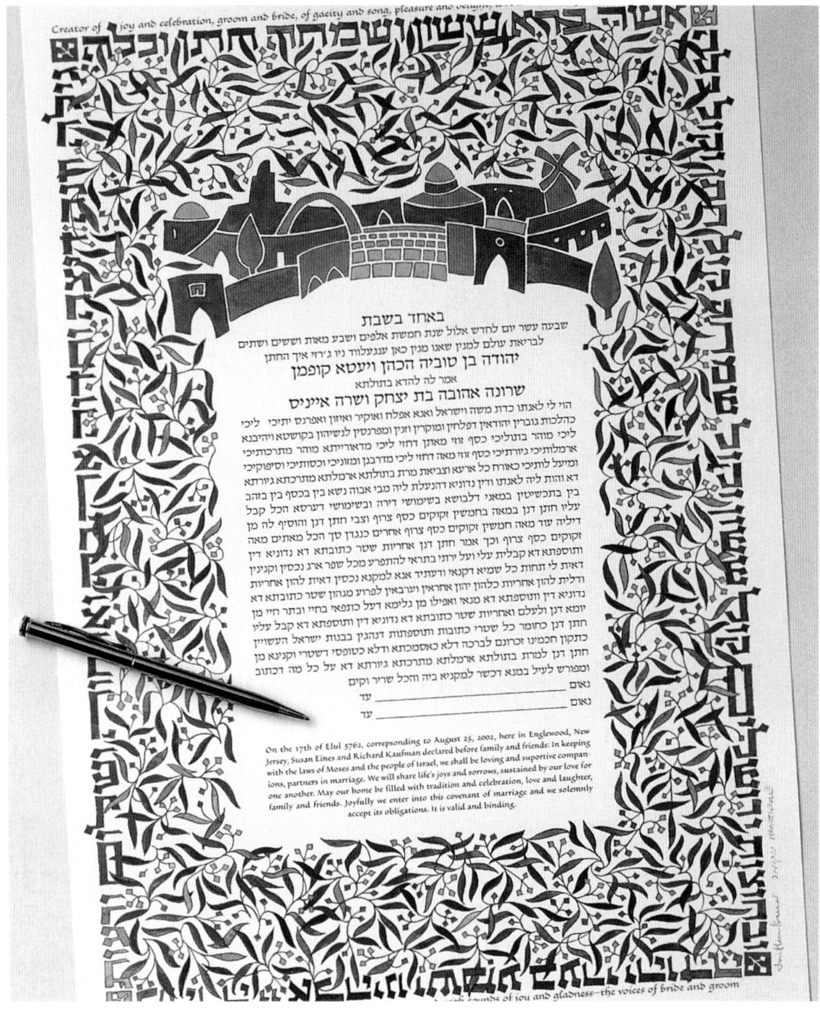

On the 17th of Elul 5762, corresponding to August 25, 2002, here in Englewood, New
Jersey, Susan Eines and Richard Kaufman declared before family and friends: In keeping
with the laws of Moses and the people of Israel, we shall be loving and suportive companions, partners in marriage. We will share life's joys and sorrows, sustained by our love for
one another. May our home be filled with tradition and celebration, love and laughter,
family and friends. Joyfully we enter into this covenant of marriage and we solemnly
accept its obligations. It is valid and binding.

❦ *ABOVE: "Gates" by Jonathan Kremer.*

❦ *OPPOSITE: A cut-paper* ketubah *by Ardyn Halter is first made entirely by hand, then cut by laser.*

THIS ONE PIECE OF PAPER IS MORE important than a knockout diamond, a beautiful wedding album, piles of gifts, or a heavenly island honeymoon. This is a gift from the husband to his wife, outlining his obligations to the woman who will share his life. It is a written document assuring respect, dignity, happiness, shelter, and legal and financial rights within the union. These are the promises of a lifetime, to be taken seriously and read aloud for the first time during the wedding ceremony for all to hear. The document is signed by both the bride and groom, and by two witnesses.

A *ketubah* was one of the earliest Jewish papers found from ancient times, somewhere between 440 and 420 B.C.E., unearthed in southern Egypt around the turn of the last century. And just forty years ago, in an Israeli cave above the Dead Sea, a woman's leather purse containing a thick bundle of ancient papyrus, included the unmistakable *ketubah* of a woman named Babta, whose contract was written sometime around 130 B.C.E.

So important were these *ketubahs* that Persian women slept with them under their pillows, tucked into silk pouches. The rabbis even decreed that a man and woman, although married, should not spend even one hour together in a home without a *ketubah*. If a *ketubah* is lost, stolen, or destroyed it is to be replaced immediately to ensure *shalom bayit,* a happy home.

Today, *ketubahs* are becoming works of art and an expression of the bride's and groom's personal tastes and preferences.

Many couples hire an artist who is also a Hebrew calligrapher to create a special work of art to hang in their home in a prominent place, proclaiming their commitment on a daily basis. The practice of creating ornately beautiful *ketubahs* is largely Sephardic in origin, and included not only a flowery written description of the bride and groom, but beautifully rendered and complicated geometrics reminiscent of the architecture in that part of the world. Still others are festooned with flowers, birds, and even zodiac signs.

European (or Ashkenazi) Jews, on the other hand, usually had very plain lettered parchments, with no adornments. During times of persecution in Europe, *ketubahs* were often crudely lettered on plain paper.

Choices range from laser-cut paper to lithography to silk-screening to original paint or colored pencils on paper. Some *ketubahs* are preprinted with the names of the bride and groom inserted in the blanks. Others are original pieces of art, with icons that are meaningful to the bride and groom incorporated into the artwork. Keep in mind that even a simple black-and-white *ketubah* can look great when beautifully custom-framed. You may want to use the design from your *ketubah* on the cover of your wedding program or invitation. Speak to the artist about getting another size of the image that you can give to your printer.

But the *ketubah* is more than a decoration or a religious document. Legend has it that when a couple quarrels, they should read their *ketubah* out loud to remind them of their devotion to each other.

The written content of a traditional *ke-*

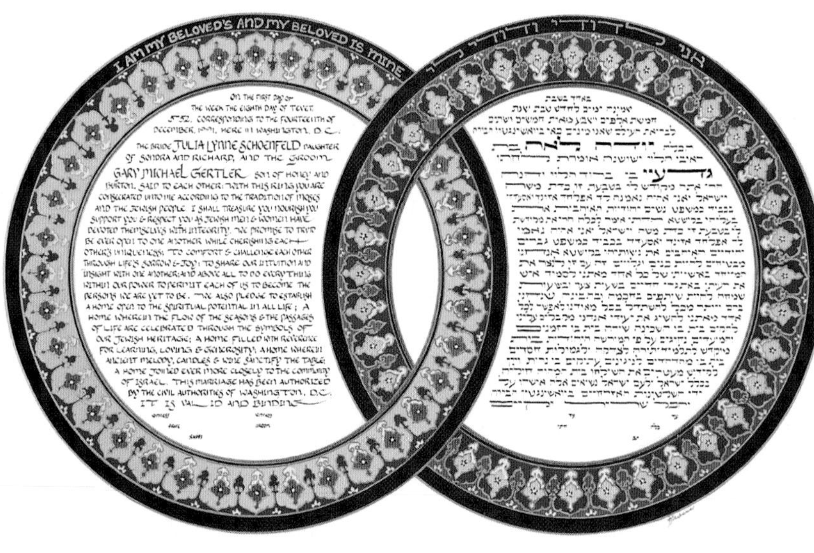

❦ OPPOSITE TOP: In Naomi Teplow's "The Four Seasons," the viewer is invited into a "Sukkah Shalom"—a Shelter of Peace.

❦ OPPOSITE BOTTOM: The "Double Ring" ketubah by Jeanette Kuvin Oren is in Hebrew and English, with gouache painting and gold-leaf embellishment.

❦ TOP LEFT: "Jerusalem Garden" by Israeli artist Ardyn Halter, who created a ketubah with a storybook look, depicts scenes from the ancient city.

❦ BELOW LEFT: The inspiration for Micah Parker's "Emanu-El" design came while he was walking to his New York hotel room past the city's Emanu-El Synagogue. The center windows in the design show the twelve tribes of Israel.

tubah has not changed much since the early centuries, but many eclectic forms are appearing today, with paragraphs that address contemporary issues. Ask your rabbi which kind is acceptable, and look at many kinds before you decide. The cost of the *ketubah* is usually the groom's choice, although the selection is a mutual choice. Our photographs of *ketubah* favorites are just a jumping-off point to a dizzying array of beautiful choices, so don't feel limited.

❦ *TOP: Laya Crust celebrates the wonders of nature with her intricate floral* ketubah *design.*

❦ *BOTTOM: William Newman burnished his "Acqui"* ketubah *with accents of 24-karat gold. His work is always hand-painted and hand-lettered to approximate the look and feel of traditional* ketubahs *from Europe and the Near East.*

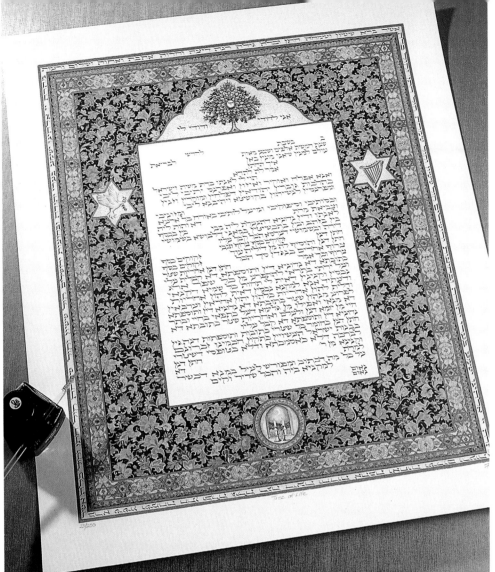

❦ *TOP: "The Tree of Life"* ketubah *by Howard Fox incorporates Jewish symbols into a richly patterned border that'sreminiscent of an Oriental carpet.*

❦ *BOTTOM LEFT: Calligrapher and artist Bobbi Yoffe designed this* ketubah *for her son's marriage. The horse near the couples' initials belongs to the groom and the covered bridge is where he proposed.*

❦ *BOTTOM RIGHT: Jonathan Kremer's "Tapestry"* ketubah *incorporates a vibrant array of Jewish artifacts with the ancient words of the* ketubah.

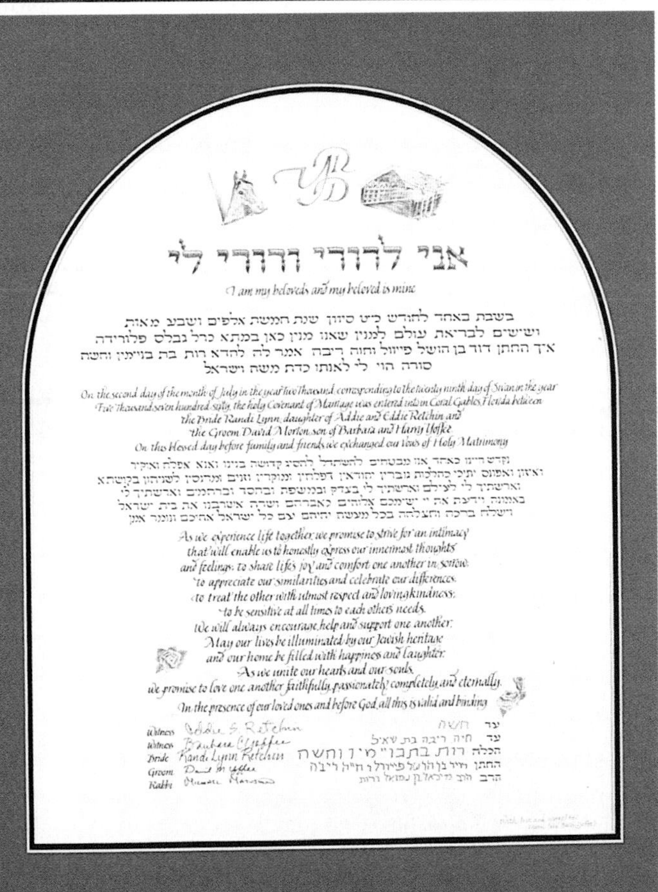

wedding invitations

❦ *OPPOSITE: Invitations with a Jewish theme are an appropriate choice for a Jewish wedding. Many traditional families often choose both Hebrew and English for the text.*

BY NOW, YOU'VE PROBABLY GUESSED that breaking the glass is the easy part of the process. Choosing the invitation that announces your decision to the world is your first public declaration, and an important one.

Of course, the invitations serve a basic purpose—to tell your guests the what, where, and when of your nuptials. But they also tell your guests a little bit about you as a couple, setting the tone for the wedding to come. Invitations have gone beyond the basic engraved look to express personal tastes, and here, we've given you some examples to get your imagination going.

PRINTING

First, you should know about the four methods of printing your invitations before you make your decision.

Engraving is the most costly of the four. Engraved invitations are usually on heavy paper, have delicate tissue slip sheets, and multiple cards, and are appropriate for formal weddings. Some words of caution, however: Changes are expensive, and the entire printing project can take up to eight weeks from submission to delivery.

Thermography has a very similar look to engraving, but is less expensive and faster to produce. Offset printing produces only flat color, but if you are using many hues or are printing on textured paper, this method is ideal. On the more eclectic side, letterpress is a lovely look. The technique involves inking a raised surface and pressing it onto the chosen paper. Letterpress is labor-intensive and requires a great deal of skill, but the results are decidedly special.

PAPER

In tandem with your printing method, consider the kind of paper you want for your invitations. Just in the past few years, paper has become varied and exciting. Vellum—semiopaque paper with a frosted finish—is back. It is used not just for overlays these days; the invitation may actually be printed on vellum, secured with an organdy or gossamer ribbon. Heavy handmade papers, unusual textures, deckled or torn edges, even fabrics are being used. Also beautiful are the new papers with pressed flowers, ferns—even confetti in a rainbow of colors.

WHERE TO BUY

Start with the stationery stores, of course—look though the seemingly endless sample books; ask for advice from an experienced salesperson who has actually seen the results of the style you are consid-

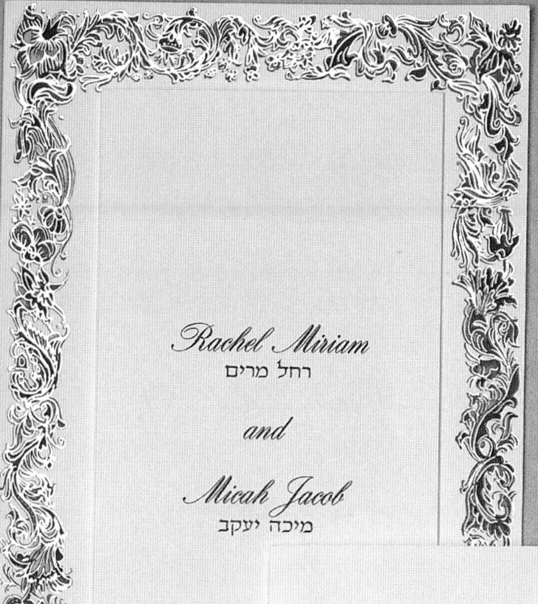
Rachel Miriam
רחל מרים
and
Micah Jacob
מיכה יעקב

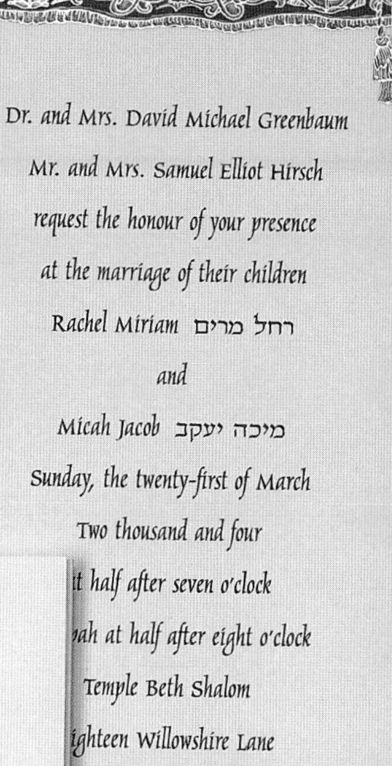
Dr. and Mrs. David Michael Greenbaum
Mr. and Mrs. Samuel Elliot Hirsch
request the honour of your presence
at the marriage of their children
Rachel Miriam רחל מרים
and
Micah Jacob מיכה יעקב
Sunday, the twenty-first of March
Two thousand and four
t half after seven o'clock
pah at half after eight o'clock
Temple Beth Shalom
ighteen Willowshire Lane
Seattle, Washington

Mrs. Rosie Applebaum
Mr. and Mrs. Alan Joshua Perlman
request the honour of your presence
at the marriage of their children
Sarah שרה
and
Mark משה
Wednesday, the twenty-fourth of October
Two thousand and seven
at six o'clock in the evening
Temple Beth Sholom
Monterey, California

בעזהשי״ת
עוד ישמע בערי יהודה ובחוצות ירושלים
קול ששון וקול שמחה
קול חתן וקול כלה
בלב מלא שמחה וברוב תודה לה׳
אנו מתכבדים להזמין את כבודכם
להשתתף בשמחת כלולות בנינו
החתן
פנחס
עב״ל
הכלה
לאה
שתתקיים אי״ה בשעה טובה ומוצלחת
יום ראשון, כ״ב סיון, תשנ״ט
קבלת פנים בשעה חמש בערב
בית הכנסת בת ציון
סקרסדיל, ניו יורק
הורי החתן
חנה ושלמה הולנדר
הורי הכלה
שרה ואריה אלטמן

Dr. and Mrs. Sheldon Kafer
request the honour of your presence
at the marriage of their daughter
Shira
to
Mr. Joel Miller
Sunday, the fourteenth of June
The year two thousand and two
at six o'clock in the evening
Emanual Temple
Shaker Heights, Ohio
Reception to follow at
Tower Ridge County Club
Nod Road
Mr. and Mrs. Larry Bramberg
request the honour of your presence
at the marriage of their daughter
Ariella Benna
to
Mr. Jeffery Alan Rosen
Sunday, April twenty-first
The year two thousand and two
at four o'clock in the afternoon
Temple Emanuel
Atlanta, Georgia
Reception afterwards at
The Atlanta Regency
request the pleasure of your company
at the marriage of their children
Ariel Renee
and
Daniel Marc
Sunday, the fifth of August
Two thousand and one
at seven past six in the evening
Temple B'Nai Jeshurun
Short Hills, New Jersey
Dr. and Mrs. Eric Platt
request the honour of your presence
at the marriage of their daughter
Carolyn Ilana
to
Mr. Michael Harold Rothstein
Sunday, the fourteenth of October
The year two thousand and one
at six o'clock in the evening
Congregation Beth El
Clayton, Missouri
Reception to follow at
The Ritz Carlton Hotel

❦ *ABOVE: Make them yourself—these invitations were printed on a home printer from kits specially made to do it yourself. Everything you need is provided—even the bows—for a truly professional look.*

❦ *OPPOSITE: Larger distinguished mills have a plethora of choices. Vellum overlays and extra touches like lavish bows are very popular. Other choices are thermography printed on simple white stock with an embossed ribbon or a pastel border for a more colorful invitation. The bottom left is an example of letterpress—relief printing directly onto paper. Since it is the oldest form of printing, it has more of an antique appearance.*

ering. Check the Web, too, since so many online stationery stores have popped up. Besides a concise, no-nonsense presentation of papers, type fonts, and inks, they will be happy to send you samples of just about anything about which you're curious. If you want something that's very personal, consider a graphic designer or even a calligrapher to help you create something special. Hebrew and English lettering can be interwoven beautifully, using a couple's name, or formed into a symbol that expresses something important to you. A leaf theme for an autumn wedding, or a hand-carved ink block on thick handmade paper tied with raffia is just another idea that can be executed by a designer, an art supply shop specializing in beautiful papers, and a printer.

HOME CREATIONS

With the dizzying variety of computer-ready papers and envelopes today, don't dismiss the possibility of doing the invitations yourself on your PC. These papers are all created to be used with a home printer, and the looks are varied and interesting. The only drawback—the ink you use will probably be black. But the upside is that as your guest list grows, the cost of the invitations won't, because you can knock off a stack in just a few minutes. Just save the layout and words in a document that's easy to pull up, and get going. Lots of these papers also come with semi-opaque vellum overlays and ribbons to give them a very professional look that's light on the pocketbook.

PERSONAL TOUCHES

When was the last time you got an invitation closed with a wax seal? It's a charming idea, and you may have your design customized. Rubber stamps can be customized for a neat look, too. Hebrew text for the cover design, again, is lovely—especially when done in micro-calligraphy, tiny Hebrew letters done by specialty artists.

SOME COMMON SENSE

Since handwork really adds to the cost of invitations, try doing some of the work yourself if you have the time. Folding, tying ribbons, inserting vellum sheets are all easy tasks that really save money at a time when everything you need suddenly costs a fortune. Remember, add backwards—count back six months when ordering invitations, and plan to have your guests receive them six to eight weeks before the wedding.

Happy is the husband of a beautiful woman, the number of his days is doubled.

~Yavamoy 63b

CHAPTER THREE

THE wedding

Weddings bring out the best in people. After all, who can sit dry-eyed through a wedding ceremony without remembering their own, or dreaming of the wedding they wish to have someday? It is an emotional time, filled with anticipation, tension, happiness, and joy. Those butterflies are real, and guests seem to get a healthy dose of them, no matter how many weddings they have attended.

What seems like a seamless, effortless ceremony to your guests—the words under the *chuppah,* the smashing of the wineglass, and finally the cries of *"Mazel tov"*—is actually a well-choreographed effort that has been planned months in advance by the two of you.

When the ceremony is finished, with its ancient words and traditions, the celebration begins—the wild spinning of the horah, the bride and groom lifted high on chairs during the dancing, the wedding meal, the toasts, the accolades, photos, laughing, wedding videos, and the centerpieces that float out the door with guests like magic.

These are the moments that make memories—for both you and your guests. We will show you how to make each moment really special, while giving you a guide to the practical as well. The Jewish wedding customs are beautiful and time-honored, and you'll benefit from adapting these to your wedding day. Use this chapter as a guide to make every aspect of your wonderful day—from processional to music, program to favors—just that: Wonderful.

where and when

Dates to Avoid

According to Jewish law, weddings are forbidden on the following days:

Sabbath

Rosh Hashanah

Yom Kippur

Sukkot

Passover

Shavuot

During the counting of the Omer (the seven weeks from Passover to Shavuot, excluding Lag B'Omer)

The three weeks from the Seventeenth of Tammuz to the Ninth of Av

The following fast days:
Tisha B'Av
Tenth of Tevet
Seventeenth of Tammuz
Fast of Gedaliah
(Third of Tishrei)
Fast of Esther
(Third of Adar)

ON A BEACH IN HAWAII. STANDING ON the ancient stones of Jerusalem's Old City. Under the *chuppah* at your family's synagogue. Or feeling the sun on your face in a field of wildflowers on Martha's Vineyard. Like most of us, you've probably had a wedding location fantasy since you were playing with Barbie dolls, and now it's finally time to decide.

Although a Jewish wedding may be held in any appropriate place, the custom among most Ashkenazi (Eastern European) and Sephardic (Middle Eastern) Jews has been to have the ceremony in a synagogue. Yes, it is a holy place, but the synagogue, especially the one you grew up in, also holds your history and that of your family. Your naming ceremony, your bar or bat mitzvah, the weddings, celebrations, and even sorrows are part of the very fabric of your being. Maybe the two of you even met there. The setting is familiar, comforting, and as dear as an old friend, and for many couples, it make sense to make those walls a part of your important day.

But there are lots of options, as you can see from the photo of an outdoor wedding with the skyline of Manhattan as a breathtaking backdrop. Keep in mind that with any outdoor event, the weather is a consideration, and the *Farmer's Almanac* isn't always reliable, nor is Doppler radar, for that matter. Even if you're planning to use tents, remember that springtime in most of the United States can be downright bone-chilling, and most guests can't show off their wedding guest finery under a trench coat.

Many weddings take place in the catering hall where the reception is to be held, which makes sense, especially in the city. In many heavily Orthodox neighborhoods in New York, for example, the actual *chuppah* ceremony is always held outside under the stars (no matter what the season), and the party moves inside afterwards. Wedding halls are booked so far in advance that weeknight weddings are common in these areas. Tuesday is a special favorite because it is considered good luck—on that day, during the creation, God said "It is good" not just once, but twice.

If you're holding the ceremony in an unusual outdoor setting, make certain to check with park rangers, the town hall, or other authorities to make sure your selection is allowed, and find out whether or not you need a temporary permit or written permission. A happy note: Once you've chosen your location, everything else begins to fall into place.

❦ *ABOVE: The Manhattan skyline makes a dramatic backdrop for this New York wedding.*

❦ *LEFT: Choose the date for your wedding carefully so that it does not interfere with Jewish holidays.*

order of the wedding

❦ ABOVE: *The signing of the* ketubah *is done shortly before the wedding ceremony.*

THE FOLLOWING PAGES PRESENT AN overview of the traditional customs and rituals of the Jewish wedding ceremony. Although not practiced uniformly by all Jews today, they present a rich array of the traditions available to every bride and groom. While the rituals and customs a couple decide to incorporate into their wedding ceremony is a very personal decision, it is one that should not be taken lightly. For the rituals not only bring aesthetic and spiritual beauty to the ceremony, some also have Jewish legal meaning and significance for the ceremony itself. The descriptions here are meant as an introduction only and will be a good preparation for working closely with your rabbi.

Before the Chuppah

FASTING

Although not required by Jewish law, couples have fasted on their wedding day for thousands of years. It is said that God forgives the couple for past deeds on their wedding day so they can start their new lives together in purity. The fast starts at sunrise and ends with the ceremony if the ceremony takes place in the daytime. However, if the ceremony is at night, the couple breaks the fast at nightfall. If one is not well or fasting is too difficult, it is a custom to give generously to charity on the wedding day instead.

PRENUPTIAL RECEPTIONS

Although this practice is not universally observed, traditional Jewish weddings begin with separate receptions for the bride and groom—the *kabbalat panim*. The bride receives her guests while seated on an elegant throne surrounded by her attendants, close family, and friends. The atmosphere is festive, with music playing and friends dancing to entertain and honor the bride. At some point the bride delivers a Torah discourse. At the very same time at the groom's reception, the *choson tish*, the groom is seated at a table, with his father, the bride's father, the rabbi, and his friends. The table, called *tish* in Yiddish, is laden with food and drink. The groom starts to deliver a Torah discourse but is immediately interrupted with joyous singing, clapping, toasting, and merriment.

WITNESSING THE *KETUBAH*

Prior to the actual ceremony, the rabbi carefully reviews the terms of the *ketubah* and the groom accepts all the terms in the following way. The rabbi, representing the bride, hands him a small article of clothing, like a handkerchief, which the groom symbolically lifts up, signaling his acceptance, and then returns to the rabbi. This procedure, called a *kinyan,* indicates formal acknowledgement of the agreement. The *kinyan* should be done in the presence of two witnesses who then sign the *ketubah*. While the *ketubah* is often signed in the rabbi's study, traditional Jews sign it at the groom's reception.

THE VEILING CEREMONY

The veiling ceremony, called *badeken* in Hebrew, is as beautiful as it is ancient. The Torah recalls that when Rebecca saw her bridegroom, Isaac, approaching "she took her veil and covered herself" as an act of modesty. The *badeken* ceremony is one of the most touching and intimate moments of the entire wedding day for the bride and groom and their parents.

The veiling ceremony begins with the groom's being led by members of his entourage to his bride, whom he now sees for the first time in her full wedding attire. He then covers her with the veil, and their parents then come together and bless her with these ancient words: "Our sister, may you become thousands of myriads." There are many variations as to who recites the blessings. This same blessing was given to Rachel over three thousand years ago. The groom is then escorted back to his area as both make their final preparations. They will next be together under the *chuppah*.

THE PROCESSIONAL

Now with the drama and flair appropriate to the event itself, the processional begins. From the assembled guests, to the rabbi and cantor under the *chuppah,* all wait with great anticipation for this moment, matchless in happiness, dignity, and beauty.

The bride and groom are royalty on their wedding day. And just as a king or queen is always accompanied by a large retinue, so are the bride and groom as they are escorted to the *chuppah*. Just before she takes her place under the *chuppah,* the bride circles the groom several times, an act rich in aesthetic and spiritual beauty. There are several common variations of how the processional takes place, giving you wide latitude to satisfy your personal desires. Please see "Wedding Processional" in this chapter for a full treatment of this subject.

Under the Chuppah

THE WELCOMING

The star of the wedding is the bride, and she takes her place last under the *chuppah,* standing to the right of the groom.

Now the cantor intones words of welcome, "Blessed is he who has come. Blessed is she who has come," formally welcoming the bride and groom and all the assembled guests. The cantor then chants a poem of praise to God, "He who is mighty over all, He who is blessed over all, He who is supreme over all, may He bless the bridegroom and the bride."

Now, all is ready for the ceremony to begin.

❦ *ABOVE: This bride's wedding ring is plain gold with no stones, in accordance with ancient tradition that the unadorned band symbolically represents the realistic attributes on which the marriage should be based.*

❦ *ABOVE: The breaking of the glass is to remind us of the destruction of the Holy Temple and Jerusalem.*

THE CEREMONY

The Jewish wedding is composed of two parts. The first is called *kiddushin,* signifying sanctification and dedication. This includes the betrothal blessings, the recitation of the marriage formula, and the giving of the ring. The second, the *nesuin,* completes the marriage ceremony and consists of the reading of the Seven Blessings, the breaking of the glass, and *yichud.* The two parts are separated by the public reading of the *ketubah* and, in most instances, the rabbi also makes his remarks at this time. In ancient times the betrothal took place in the bride's parents' home and the *nesuin* a year later in that of the groom. The year between was like today's engagement period, except that the couple lived apart and were not entitled to conjugal rights. Later on, in times of persecution, couples sometimes became permanently separated during that year. To avoid this the rabbis joined the two ceremonies together to be performed consecutively under the *chuppah* as we still practice today.

PART ONE: THE *KIDDUSHIN*

The rabbi first recites the blessing over wine, which in Judaism represents joy and happiness. The rabbi then recites the betrothal blessing, which praises God for the gift of marriage. The groom and bride then drink from the cup.

Next the groom is to place the ring on the bride's finger. The procedure is as follows: The groom honors two guests by asking them to be witnesses. The rabbi shows them the ring and asks them if it has the value of a perutah, an ancient coin worth about two cents today. They are to answer yes. The rabbi asks the groom if the ring belongs to him. The groom then takes the ring and recites the ancient marriage formula, "Behold, you are consecrated to me with this ring in accordance with the laws of Moses and Israel." This should be done in both Hebrew and English. Then, the groom places the ring on the bride's right forefinger, as the right side symbolizes love. She may move it to her ring finger after the ceremony.

The essence of the ceremony is the groom's giving of a gift—the ring—to the bride and her acceptance of it. For this reason the ring must belong to the groom. A double-ring ceremony causes problems in Halacha, Jewish law, as the rings would then be considered an exchange and the bride's ring not a gift. If it is desired that the man wear a ring, he can simply be given one later on after the ceremony.

The rabbi then reads the *ketubah* and gives it to the groom who hands it to the bride. The *kiddushin,* the first part of the ceremony, is now completed. Although many rabbis make their remarks at this point, this is really up to the discretion of the rabbi and the couple. The first part of the ceremony is now complete.

PART TWO: THE NESUIN

The second part of the ceremony consists of the reading of the Seven Blessings, the breaking of the glass, and *yichud.* In many weddings the rabbi or cantor recites all the blessings. At traditional and Hasidic weddings, close family members and honored guests are asked to do so, and this is considered a great honor.

THE SEVEN BLESSINGS

The first blessing is the blessing over wine.

The second blesses God for creating the world "Who created all things for His glory." The third and fourth thank God for making us in His image. Because God gave us free will, we have the ability to emulate God by doing acts of kindness. The fifth blessing is for Jerusalem and Zion. It recalls Jerusalem's destruction and refers to the future when the Jewish people will eventually return in joy. The sixth and seventh blessings refer to the bride and groom as "beloved companions" and asks that God grant them "joy and happiness, rejoicing and song, delight and good cheer, love and harmony, peace and friendship."

After the final words of the Seven Blessings, the groom and bride drink from the second cup of wine, and the wedding ceremony has been completed.

The wedding ceremony passes quickly by but touches on the greatest of themes. God has been petitioned to shower them with blessings for a good and happy life. The couple have been reminded that they are an important part of the fabric of the Jewish people, and that according to the laws of Moses and Israel they have now been made holy to each other.

BREAKING THE GLASS

A glass goblet is then wrapped and placed at the foot of the groom, who then proceeds to step on it, shattering the glass. This is followed by shouts of "*Mazel tov.*" This ritual is to remind of us of the destruction of Jerusalem and the Holy Temple, which we should recall even at our happiest of moments.

After the Chuppah

YICHUD

With the shattering of the glass, the quiet movement of the wedding ceremony is soon swept away in celebration. A wonderful custom, the *yichud,* ensures that the couple's first moments as husband and wife are spent together privately. Friends escort the couple to a private room where a table is set with a snack and bottle of champagne or wine. In those precious moments the couple gets to share their thoughts and feelings, and, most of all, their happiness. Although many consider *yichud* a custom, in traditional circles it is considered a necessary part of the wedding.

❦ *ABOVE: The bride and groom will appreciate a beautiful* yichud *table for two, complete with champagne, pâté, and truffles.*

❦ *OPPOSITE PAGE: The wedding processional, simplified. The rabbi and cantor lead, followed by both sets of grandparents. Next come the best man and ushers and then the groom and his parents. The bridesmaids, maid or matron of honor, and flower girl follow. Finally, the bride is ushered to the* chuppah *by her parents—mother on the right, father on the left.*

❦ *TOP, THIS PAGE: The correct positioning of the wedding party under the* chuppah. *Only the bride and groom must stand under the* chuppah. *If the* chuppah *is too small to accommodate everyone, the wedding party may stand just outside.*

❦ *BOTTOM, THIS PAGE: The first few rows of the seating are reserved for the grandparents, special friends, and family—on the left for the groom's, right for the bride's.*

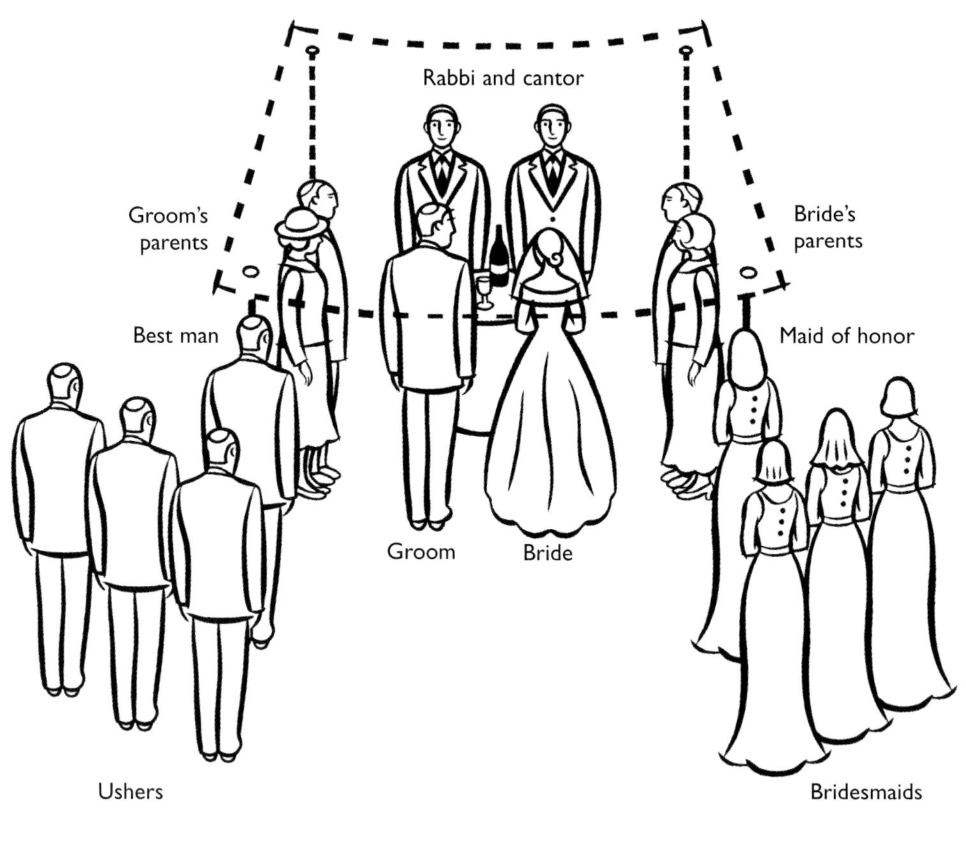

wedding processional

THERE IS A JEWISH TRADITION THAT the last is always the most precious. So just as Adam waited for Eve in the Garden of Eden, the groom still takes his place first under the *chuppah* to await the arrival of his bride.

Tradition relates that it was God who escorted Eve to the *chuppah,* while Adam's escorts were the angels Michael and Gabriel. Since that first wedding, attendants continue to escort the couple, considered as royalty, to the site of their sacred union.

There are no hard-and-fast rules concerning who escorts the couple to the *chuppah.* In many weddings, the groom is escorted by his parents, and the bride by hers. In many traditional and Hasidic circles, both fathers escort the groom and both mothers the bride. In Jewish practice there is no "giving away" of the bride by her father, rather her parents bring her to the *chuppah,* which is considered the groom's domain.

As in the traditional American wedding, the Jewish wedding party starts down the aisle right foot first. The rabbi and the cantor lead the procession, followed by the bride's grandparents, and then the groom's. While many Jewish weddings follow American practice by having the ushers and bridesmaids follow next paired together, this is not done in traditional Jewish weddings. Instead the ushers and best man come next, followed in order by the bridesmaids, maid or matron of honor, and flower girls, and then the bride is escorted by her parents.

Once up the aisle, most members of the wedding party stand under the *chuppah* with the bride and groom. If the *chuppah* is not large enough to accommodate everyone, attendants may stand just outside the *chuppah.* Seating is usually provided in the front rows for the grandparents and those who may need it.

Before taking her place under the *chuppah,* the bride walks around the groom several times, creating symbolic circles. She then steps inside the circles symbolizing the creation of their new bond of marriage, forever to be protected by walls of love and commitment. Depending on family or community tradition, this is done either three or seven times. Three represents the husband's obligation to provide his wife with sustenance, clothing, and conjugal rights. Seven has many mystical connotations—one being to recall the seven days of creation.

The variations in the wedding processional give you license to choose the one that is most pleasing. Under the *chuppah,* the words and ceremony that make the couple husband and wife have remained virtually unchanged for thousands of years.

sacred spaces: *chuppahs*

❦ *OPPOSITE: This rustic willow* chuppah *frame was commissioned from an artist who specializes in Adirondack-style furniture. The poles are screwed into platforms and secured into the ground with stakes. For contrast, the top is draped with a sheer white cloth.*

WHETHER OF SIMPLE OR ELABORATE design, the *chuppah* is among the most beautiful and charming of all Jewish customs. Although the entire wedding ceremony takes place under it, the *chuppah*, is not simply a tradition—it is an essential part of the wedding ceremony itself. The *chuppah* is a public declaration that the couple now stand under one roof for the first time as husband and wife. And it is also symbolic of the new home they will establish as a married couple.

It is said during this sacred time, as the bride stands under the *chuppah*, she may ask God for special favors, for herself and for others. In fact, at many traditional weddings today, the bride is asked to request speedy recoveries, easy births, and relief from difficult situations from family members and friends.

If you plan to create your own *chuppah*, only a few rules apply. The four sides must be completely open, as a nod of respect to Abraham, who was famous for inviting wayfarers and guests to his tent—he kept all four tent sides open so that guests would not have to search for his door. This is a reminder to the new couple that their home should always be open to guests as well.

The traditional *chuppah* is often a tallis, or other piece of cloth, attached to the tops of four poles which can be self-supporting, or held aloft over the couple by four friends. If you would like the poles to stand alone, mix up a batch of quick-drying concrete—the kind used for backyard swing sets and garden arbors—pour it into four large containers (buckets or flowerpots work well), and insert the poles. "Bag" the buckets with gold lamé and tie them with ribbons, or at a more informal wedding, paint the buckets and affix them with chunks of beach glass, pebbles, marbles, or even colorful broken tiles.

Now for the *chuppah* design. As a gesture of love and respect, many couples use a plain tallis from a loved one who has passed away, but the ideas are as numerous as the stars in the sky, also. A lovely idea would be to use trains or veils from a mother's or grandmother's wedding to form the canopy. An heirloom or crocheted bedspread or table covering would be equally beautiful. There are Judaica artists who specialize in *chuppahs* and will create a custom design for you—maybe a delicate hand-painted silk, or batik. It is considered a *hiddur mitzvah* (to perform a mitzvah in the most aesthetically attractive manner possible) to create the most beautiful *chuppah* you can. Don't forget—many synagogues have standard *chuppahs* that you may decorate with ribbons, trailing ivy, and flowers.

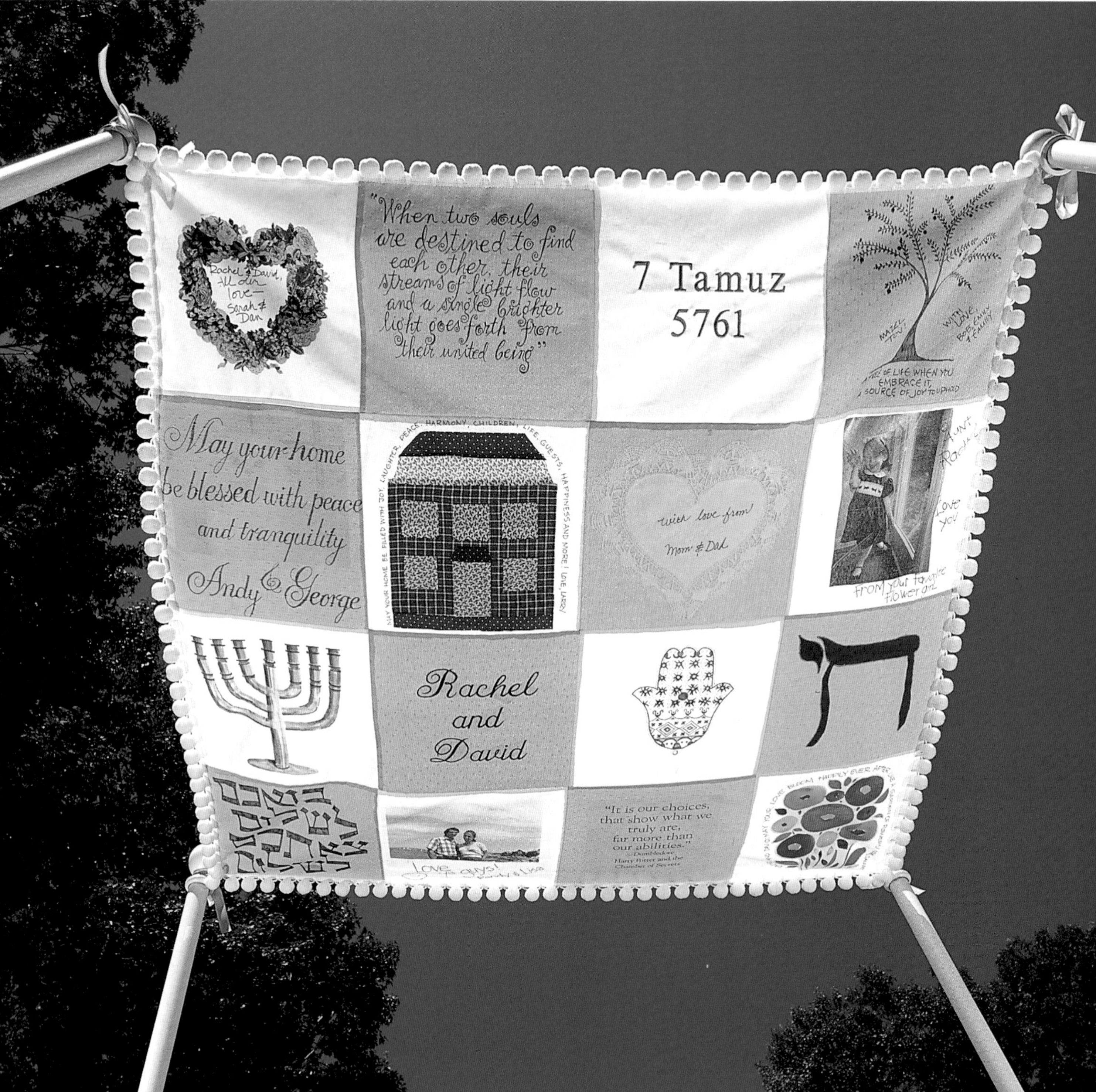

❦ *ABOVE: Everyone gets into the act to create an heirloom patchwork-quilt* chuppah *that may be used for an eclectic, one-of-a-kind wall hanging.*

❦ *OPPOSITE: Birds fly over the couple on a* chuppah *trimmed in lime green and orange.*

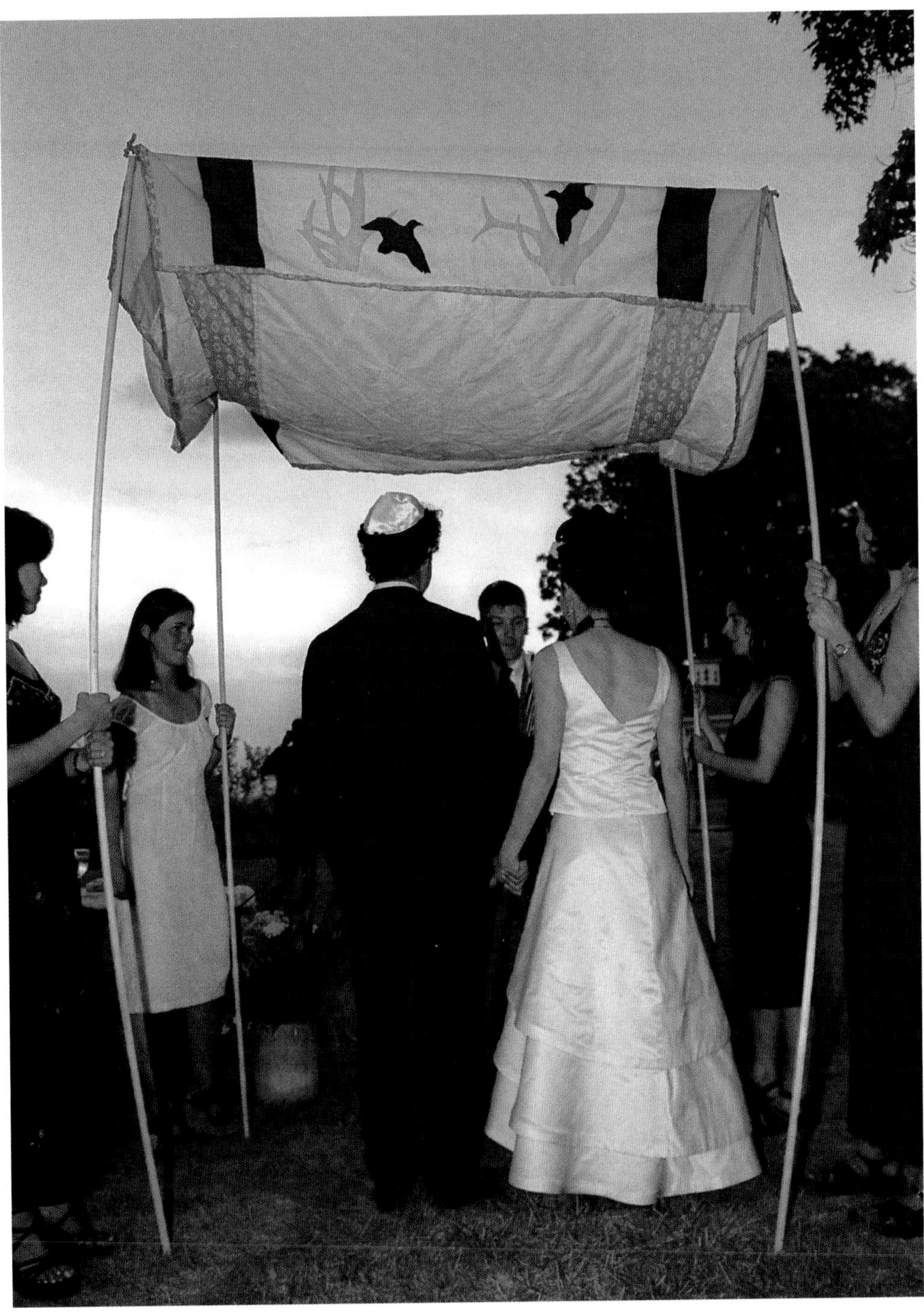

Chuppah Ideas

If your wedding ceremony is at night, try wrapping tiny white or blue holiday lights around the supports and frame of your *chuppah*. This look is so striking that not much more decoration is really needed. You can also punctuate the aisle with simple luminaries made with white paper bags, filled with sand and some votives.

Flowers can transform a plain *chuppah* into something quite spectacular. Remember, the roof must still be fabric.

Use ribbons lavishly to add Victorian romance to your *chuppah*. They can wrap around the poles, as on a maypole, as well as crisscrossing on plain white fabric.

Painting on silk is easy if you use paint made specifically for silk. A silk *chuppah* is very delicate looking but quite strong.

Unattractive poles can be covered with silk ivy, yards of tulle, or ropes of real flowers.

A family "quilt" makes a colorful, unique *chuppah* that becomes an instant heirloom, as pictured here. Choose sixteen or so people to each create a square, then have the squares sewn together with a heavy blanket stitch, and have loops made for the poles. You may use the loops with a hanging rod as a special piece of artwork for your new home together. Just remember to keep your *chuppah* design in direct line with the wedding style you've chosen so that the look blends in well on this special day.

❦ *ABOVE: White satin is appropriate for a formal wedding, even for the* chuppah. *The bride's late father's tallis was incorporated into the* chuppah *to honor his memory.*

❦ *OPPOSITE: This luxe look was created with a velvety canopy and gold-leaf finials. The poles are actually white closet dowels that are sprayed gold and cemented into clay pots topped with moss. Tassels are the finishing touch for this elegant Renaissance look.*

אנכי
לא יהיה
לא תשא
זכור את
כבד את
לא תרצח
לא תנאף
לא תגנב
לא תענה
לא תחמד

music to your ears

Some of Our Favorites

The Ceremony
"Al Kol Ele"
"Jerusalem of Gold"
"Erev Shel Shoshanim"
"Erev Ba"
"Dodi Li"

Entrance of the Bride and Groom
"Oseh Shalom"
"Asher Bara"
"Od Yishama"

Dancing
"Artsa Alinu"
"Hava Nagila"
"Rad Halaila"

Israeli Dance Music
"Hine Ma Tov"
"Mayim, Mayim"
"Tzena Tzena"

Klezmer Music
"Mezinka"
"Chosen Kale Mazel Tov, Siman Tov"

WHEN THE MUSIC AT A JEWISH wedding is of a sacred nature, then so is the wedding itself. The concept is far from new—the Torah mentions music at wedding ceremonies. So when you are escorted to meet your *barshert* to the strains of your carefully chosen music, you're walking to the tune of history.

That doesn't mean that your choices can't reflect your personality and your spirit. If you're hiring a band, discuss your preferences with the bandleader. Allow this seasoned professional to guide you through the complexities of choosing processional, ceremonial, and recessional music, since there must be a seamless flow.

A few things to remember: A sign of respect and love for those in your wedding party is to choose special processional songs—one for the groom, one for the bride, another for the parents, and a selection for the collective attendants. Ask them to suggest some of their favorites to include them in the process.

After the ceremony, be certain to instruct your musicians to continue playing until every guest has left the room. Nothing is worse than having departing guests stranded in the aisles in abrupt silence.

Now, a word of caution. It may surprise you to know that there are certain popular wedding Processional tunes that are totally inappropriate for Jewish weddings. "The Wedding March" (commonly known as "Here Comes the Bride") was written by a staunch anti-Semite, Richard Wagner. Another to avoid is the traditional American recessional music. It was written by Felix Mendelssohn and was in celebration of a pagan wedding; as such it is antithetical to the spirit of Judaism.

But whether you choose a string quartet for an elegant, dreamy mood, or the infectious, "let's celebrate" lilt of a klezmer band, is up to you. Klezmer music, once abandoned by new immigrants as being too "old world," has bounced back joyously. Klezmer music originated in the shtetels, the close-knit Jewish villages of Eastern Europe before World War II. It is enjoying an enormous revival today bringing traditional *ruach* (spirit) to *simchas,* especially weddings.

In some Orthodox and Hasidic weddings, rowdy, happy crowds of singing men escort the groom to the *chuppah* in a sea of black coats and hats. It's very spiritual, and there's not a musician in sight.

Take your time. Ask for tapes, videos, suggestions, references. Then, once you've narrowed your choices, visit an event to hear each one. Music is the language of the soul—choose music that will reflect your thoughts and feelings.

SHMELKIE'S NIGUN
S. Brazil
©by the author
KETSAD M'RAKDIN
Traditional
34
YISRAEL CHAI
S. Rockoff
HYUN

מזל טוב
כלה
מזל טוב
חתן

best seat in the house

HIGH, DRAPED, PEACOCK, OR PAINTED—special chairs for the special couple have been a tradition for centuries in Jewish weddings. These seats are actually thrones, of a sort, in keeping with the comparison of the wedding couple to royalty, and the idea that they are specially blessed and very different from their guests on this one day in their lives.

You will always find the bride before a traditional wedding seated in a high rattan peacock chair, called a *kiskallah,* surrounded by her standing mother, mother-in-law, and friends, receiving a long line of well-wishing women friends and relatives. It is an occasion for a personal word of encouragement, love, best wishes—even advice before the hectic pace to follow. The bride is almost always inaccessible after the *chuppah,* and between the music, singing, clapping, toasts and enthusiastic dancing, the din makes conversation all but impossible.

In these same groups, the groom, simultaneously, has a party for his male friends in another room, where he sits in a special chair as well, until he is escorted to the *chuppah.*

From one end of the Jewish spectrum to the other, chairs elevate the status of the betrothed couple. During the wedding meal, the bride and groom often have special seating, at a head table, facing their guests. During the dancing, chairs rise to the occasion as the bride and groom are lifted high on their seats while family and friends dance around them.

This is where your personal taste comes in, and we've provided a glimpse into the possibilities. The only limits are your imagination, and your dream of a wedding day that's perfect in every way.

❦ *OPPOSITE: Artistic friends may wish to create your first heirlooms—a pair of hand-decorated chairs, using paint, découpage, hand lettering, photos, tassels, and trim.*

❦ *TOP RIGHT: A treasured chair from home is dressed for the bride in yards of casually draped and tied tulle.*

❦ *BOTTOM RIGHT: A silk-draped banquet chair is an elegantly tailored look. Just wrap, fold, pin, and decorate with flowers, real or silk.*

THE MARRIAGE OF
MINA COHEN
AND
ADAM SCHNEIDER
SUNDAY

wedding programs

JUST AS A PLAYBILL IS THE PROGRAM for a Broadway show, your wedding program works the same way. First, it is a lasting memento of a special day. It is also a lovely way to introduce the members of your wedding party, out-of-town guests, grandparents, and other loved ones. It's a nice little extra that shows your attention to detail.

Although it is not a necessity, a program is the perfect way to explain the traditions surrounding a Jewish wedding. After all, not all of your guests will be Jewish, and they will feel more connected to your ceremony if they don't have to guess what is taking place, or continually ask other guests.

Some programs are simple and straightforward. They list the bride's and groom's names followed by the date and location. Others may give a brief description of the bridal party and their relationship to the bride or groom.

Some dedicate a memorial page to departed close relatives. Your wedding program may also serve as a charming way to immortalize your special love story. Use a panel or page to tell everyone how you met. Include your story (humor is okay) and your favorite candid photo. You may want to include a favorite poem or quote, or thank your parents or other people who helped make this day special.

The programs shown on the left are a simple solution. The shape is vertical—easy because standard paper measures 8½ by 11 inches. A sturdy stock can be found at any copy center, in a wide variety of colors. Score and fold the cover paper in half lengthwise; then get to work on your text.

Using your computer, type your cover and then the body of your program to fit within the width of your paper. For the covers, use your Copy and Paste features to make as many copies on the page as possible. Then take a printout to your copy center and ask for copies on clear overhead-transparency sheets. Make as many as you need; have them center trim the copies for you (usually at one dollar a cut) and spray the backs with an all-purpose adhesive. When they are dry, just position them on your programs and you're almost finished.

Create a tied closure by punching holes as shown, and tie a pretty bow with gossamer-sheer ribbon.

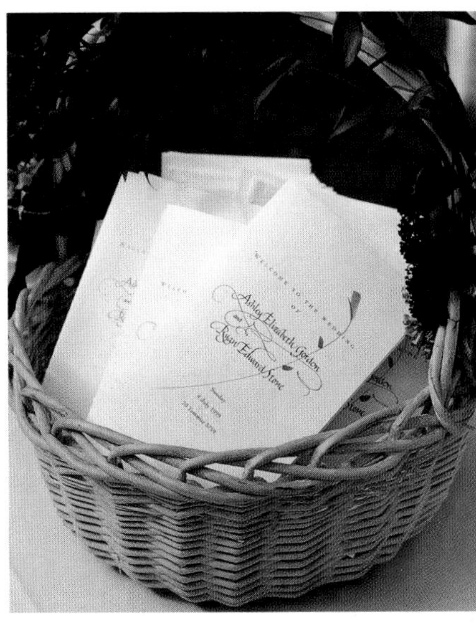

❦ *OPPOSITE: Long and narrow shapes are not only easy to produce but also economical.*

❦ *ABOVE: Printed programs are nestled in a wicker basket, ready to be picked up by the guests.*

❦ RIGHT: A four-paneled accordion-fold program is created from a single, long sheet of paper.

❦ OPPOSITE, CLOCKWISE FROM TOP LEFT: A page dedicated to the memory of those who are deceased is always appreciated by other family members; using a gold rubber stamp pad and a stencil, these initials have the appearance of being printed on; introducing your wedding party in a program is an excellent way for everyone to know who's who; skeletal leaves from the craft store are an easy way to personalize a program.

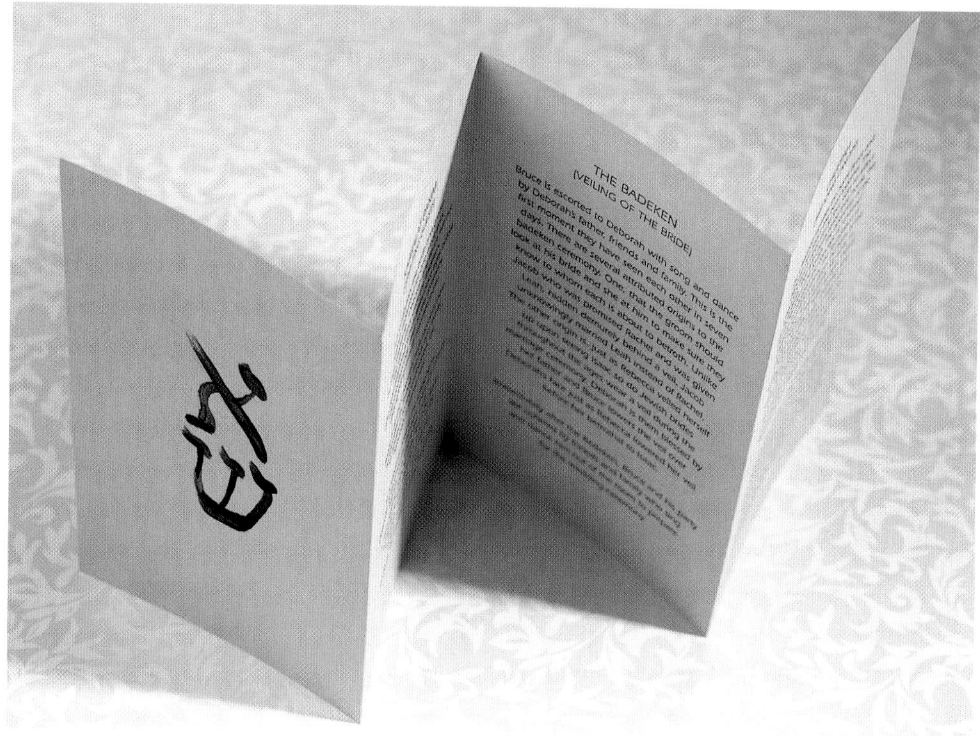

The folded design shown here has a spare, Oriental feel. The Hebrew initials on the cover have been brushed to give them a hand-painted look. On this program, the customs of a traditional Jewish wedding are explained in sequence on each panel. Display them prominently as guests enter the wedding site so they will take one to their seats. Ours includes the *kabbalat panin,* the greeting of the guests, which makes it even more important to make the program available before the ceremony.

The top right design on the opposite page just looks difficult. Using two kinds of paper—an outside heavy stock and standard white paper for the pages inside—the look is enhanced with gold initials fashioned from stencils found at a craft store. Buy a metallic gold stamp pad and you're ready to create these beautiful covers, using a sponge with the stencils for an antiqued look. The strip below the initials was done on a computer, in reverse type—black background, white lettering.

To apply, just cut out the strip with an X-Acto knife, put all-purpose spray adhesive on the back, and affix it to the cover. Add a tassel for a dramatic, elegant touch.

Naturals are always in fashion. The unusual program shown bottom left on the opposite page, combines two paper colors with a skeleton leaf (available in bags of twenty from craft stores) on the front. It is wrapped with a strip announcing the event, the bride and groom, and the date. The strip was created on the ever-faithful computer, wrapped around the entire cover, and glued into place. Natural raffia is run through the two punched holes for a lovely finishing touch.

These ideas are like a buffet—choose what you like for a program that satisfies your personal wishes. Add what you like, improvise on the designs, enlist the help of a friend or two, and you can create wedding programs as unique as you are.

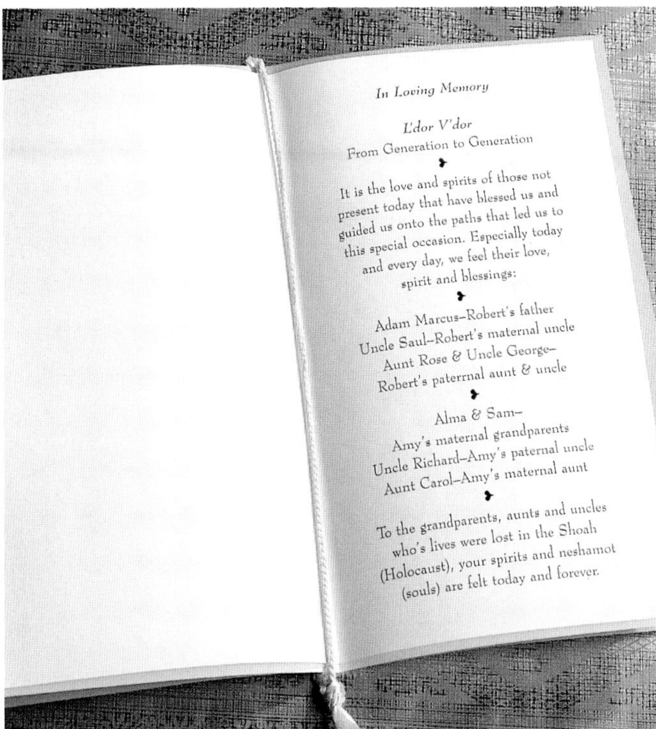
In Loving Memory
L'dor V'dor
From Generation to Generation
It is the love and spirits of those not present today that have blessed us and guided us onto the paths that led us to this special occasion. Especially today and every day, we feel their love, spirit and blessings:
Adam Marcus–Robert's father
Uncle Saul–Robert's maternal uncle
Aunt Rose & Uncle George–Robert's paternal aunt & uncle
Alma & Sam–Amy's maternal grandparents
Uncle Richard–Amy's paternal uncle
Aunt Carol–Amy's maternal aunt
To the grandparents, aunts and uncles who's lives were lost in the Shoah (Holocaust), your spirits and neshamot (souls) are felt today and forever.

AR
Amy Rosenberg & Robert Marcus

Lisa Shapiro & David Resnick
26th Day of AV, 5760

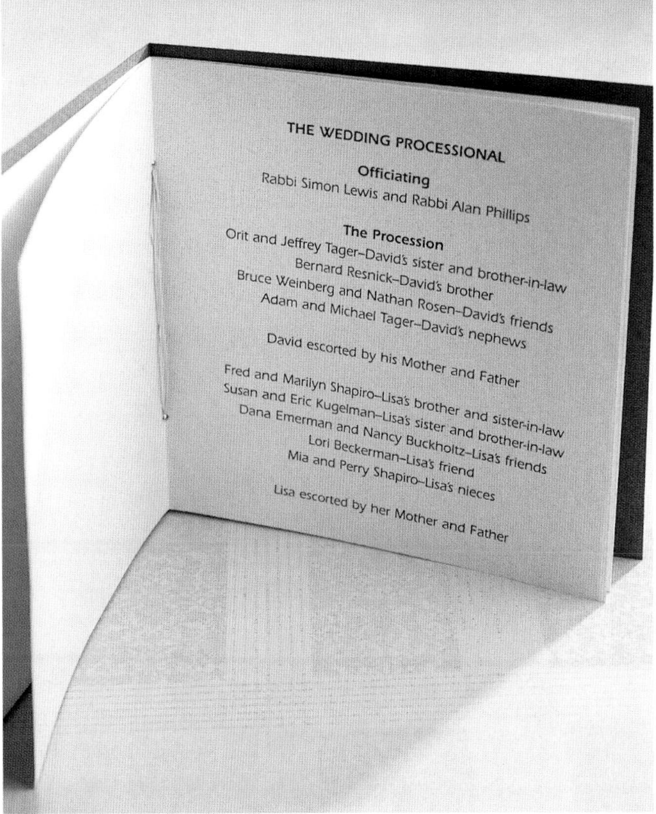
THE WEDDING PROCESSIONAL
Officiating
Rabbi Simon Lewis and Rabbi Alan Phillips
The Procession
Orit and Jeffrey Tager–David's sister and brother-in-law
Bernard Resnick–David's brother
Bruce Weinberg and Nathan Rosen–David's friends
Adam and Michael Tager–David's nephews
David escorted by his Mother and Father
Fred and Marilyn Shapiro–Lisa's brother and sister-in-law
Susan and Eric Kugelman–Lisa's sister and brother-in-law
Dana Emerman and Nancy Buckholtz–Lisa's friends
Lori Beckerman–Lisa's friend
Mia and Perry Shapiro–Lisa's nieces
Lisa escorted by her Mother and Father

❦ *CLOCKWISE FROM TOP LEFT: Clear acetate name cards sit on a thick glass cutting board; an heirloom silver tray makes an elegant holder for yarmulkahs at a formal evening wedding; an elegant wrap with a simple linen napkin contains the wineglass to be crushed by the groom (we've added a ribbon and a rose); use patterned papers made for scrapbooking as a background for seating cards; a beautiful willow basket holds yarmulkahs for a summer outdoor wedding; slip the groom's wineglass into a gauzy organza favor bag for a no-mess, elegant look that's tied at the stem.*

details make a difference

THE LITTLE THINGS MEAN A LOT. Special details have the ability to elevate an occasion and turn it into a long-lasting memory with unforgettable small touches that show how much you care for your guests.

Start early. Tuck a spiral notebook into your bag. As you get inspiration from magazines, a walk in the park, or a stroll through the mall, jot down your ideas, and you'll have lots to choose from when it's time to decide.

Of course, you know the basics: yarmulkahs look special when offered on a silver tray or in a wicker basket. Silky ribbons can be wired around wineglass stems. Pretty packaging can house necessities for the rest rooms—how about a hatbox to hold everything, or an antique wire plant stand?

Welcome baskets or bags are a must for out-of-towners staying in hotels nearby. In addition to bottled water, teas, cookies, nuts, and fruits, add a bottle of wine and a scented candle. (Don't forget a box of wooden matches.) Sightseeing guides are a thoughtful tuck-in, too.

Using valet parking? Have the attendants leave a thank-you note on the dash, along with a bag of dinner mints.

It's your wedding, and the extra little touches are all yours.

❦ *ABOVE: Baskets of wheat grass are lovely spring place-card holders, and they're easy to grow from seed. Start them one or two weeks before the wedding.*

Happy Happy Life! -Lisa + Fred

Jen + Ben

ALL THE BEST FOR A HAPPY MARRIAGE!
WITH LOVE, SARAH + JOE

A.B. + M.K.

Mazel Tov
Love,
Carol & Steve

Love
Joel + Aunt Marcy

Rabbi & Blumie Samuels

Good Luck -
May you both have
many years of
happiness.
Beth & Don

Love you guys!
Shira & David

Lots and
lots of
children
-Estelle
and

Bud

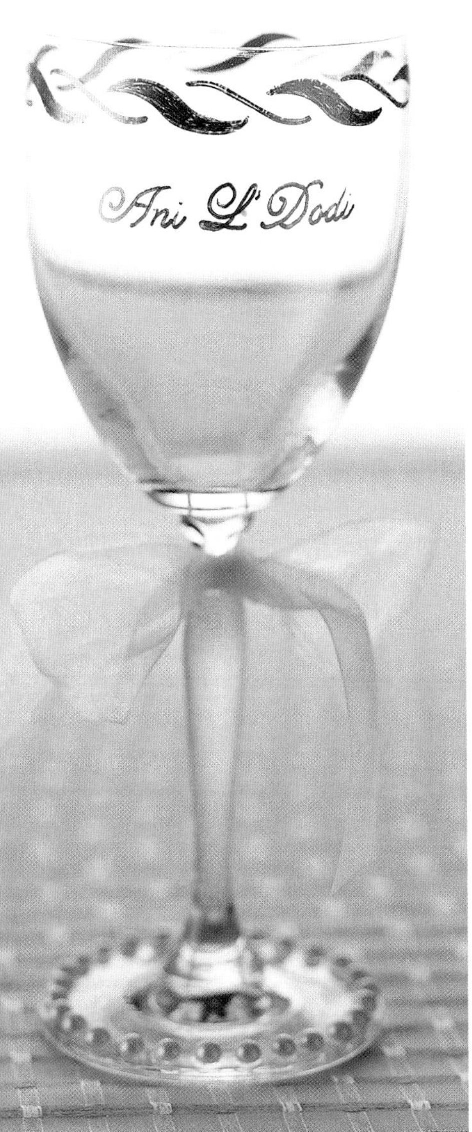

❦ *CLOCKWISE FROM TOP LEFT: Place a basket filled with necessities in the ladies' washroom. Fill with a mini sewing kit, extra panty hose, hair spray, and hand cream; napkins are the perfect place to show your creativity—a creamy rose tied with copper ribbon makes a beautiful presentation; try an olive branch wrapped around each napkin—you can order olive branches from your florist or use silk look-alikes; it's easy to personalize plain paper cocktail napkins with rubber stamps; a plain wine goblet can be transformed into a special Kiddush cup for the bride and groom with gems, glass paint and a sheer ribbon.*

❦ *OPPOSITE: Instead of a standard guest book, try a plate that your guests sign. Use metallic paint pens, and remember not to use the plate for food. It makes a nice addition hung on a wall in your first home.*

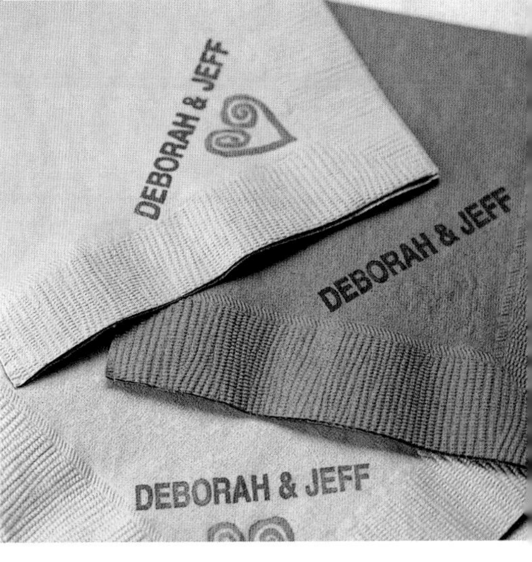

favor your guests

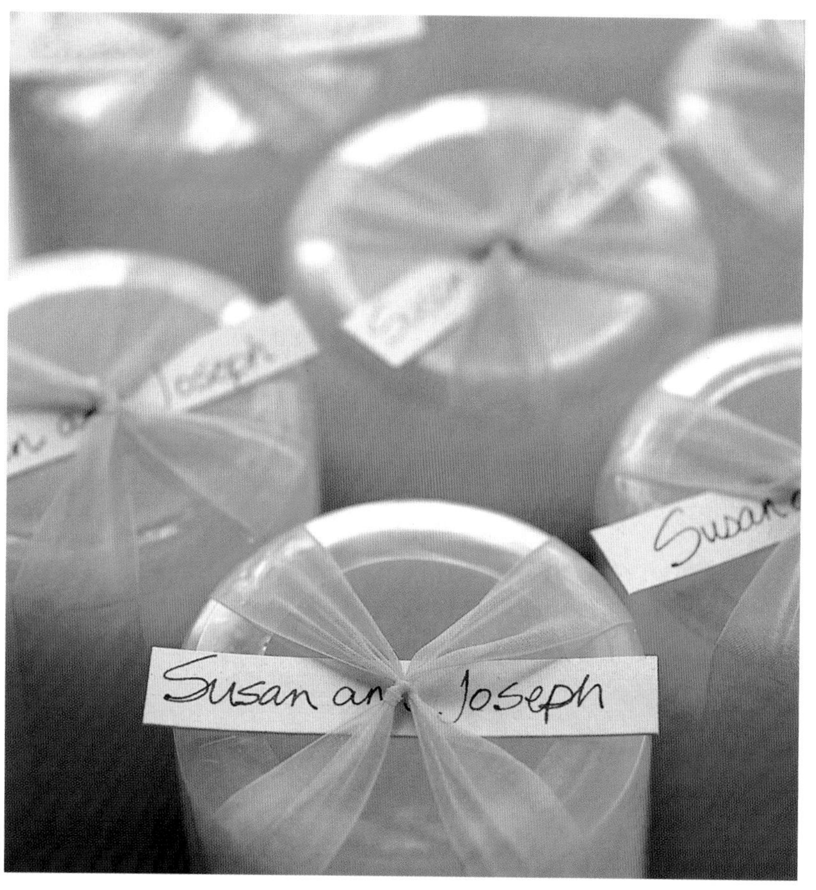

❦ *ABOVE: Chunky candles are a thoughtful and beautiful favor.*

❦ *OPPOSITE, CLOCKWISE FROM TOP LEFT: A special hand-chosen collection of songs inexpensively burned onto CDs is a unique party favor; any flavorful gift looks elegant when tucked into plain white boxes and tied simply with thick satin ribbon held in place with stickers bearing the couple's initials; colorful glycerine soaps look extra special in transparent organza bags; clear plastic boxes from the sports card store hold candies beautifully; try grown-up lollipops shaped in the initials of the bride and groom; paperwhite bulbs are a good winter choice—add pebbles from the pet shop and pop into vellum bags.*

FAVORS ARE A SPECIAL WAY TO thank your guests for coming to your wedding. They're a lovely, unexpected treat, and add lots of pizzazz to the table décor. Try something different for a change—burning CDs with a special collection of meaningful songs is a lovely idea. You can even have the valet parker tuck them as a surprise on the front seat. Luxurious soaps, flower seeds for spring, and bulbs for winter forcing are fun choices.

Now for food favors. Organic seeds, nuts—even a special trail mix are perennial favorites. How about fortune cookies with humorous personalized fortunes? Candy is a favorite—some companies even personalize your chocolates with the bride's and groom's initials; truffles are an elegant treat, and pastel Jordan almonds are a classic with their crunchy candy coating. They're nonmelting, too, for a hot summer's day. Unique lollipops are available, featuring grown-up flavors like mango, rosemary mint, and even curry. Check your local gourmet food store.

Whatever you choose, it's your way of showing how much you appreciate and love your guests on your most important day.

Lea & Jared's Favorites
June 17, 2001 • 26 Sivan 5761
B
Thank you for sharing this day with us!
A token
this happy
J S
Judy and Steve Pomerantz
14 ELUL 5762
Carol & Mark
August 3, 2002

Elana & Michael
18, 2001
2

at the center of it all

CENTERPIECES ARE STORYTELLERS. Centerpieces are eye candy. They serve as the focal point of your wedding tables and set the mood for the occasion, providing a sort of home base for guests throughout the festivities—between dances, courses, toasts, and those endless bouts of pleasurable schmoozing.

Let's talk about table shape first and what goes with what. At long, elegant banquet-style tables, low symmetrical floral arrangements and dozens upon dozens of tiny candles create a carpet-like elegance from any angle. "Lush" and "lavish" are keywords for round tables. Heap the centers with tumbling, overflowing gatherings of the season's best: Trails of fresh ivy, mounds of fall pumpkins and gourds, wild summer grapes with beach roses and pampas plumes, sweet and tender spring grasses and bulb flowers—you get the idea. A mix of either fruit and vegetables or fruits mixed with flowers is a wonderful way for nature to create a colorful and abundant focus.

A word about light, then height. Make sure you use lots of soft illumination—everyone knows how candles love a wedding, creating a soft, flattering glow. Everyone looks more radiant—and maybe that's why so many couples find each other at friends' weddings. About height: Keep your centerpieces either quite low or very high, on wrought iron or brass stands made specifically for the purpose of allowing guests to see and talk to their tablemates. (By the way, this is a wonderful way to bring an intimidatingly high ceiling down in proportion with the rest of the room.) For lower centerpieces, the general rule is a maximum of fourteen inches in height.

Flower choices? Be brave, even with your use of traditional wedding blooms. Roses are a timeless favorite, but think of topiary rose trees, streaming golden ribbons, maypole-style. Carnations may seem ho-hum, but consider these long-lived spicy beauties tightly packed together in a perfect rectangle—very country French. Don't stick to pastels, either, if you love hot pinks, bold purples and passionate oranges. Pretty pots of fresh herbs for a summer wedding are earthy and easily accessible, and scent the air with a heady freshness.

Go clean and dramatic, like the table pictured on the opposite page. All the clear glass containers match, and each is filled with the same fruits or flowers. Candles are secured in similar glass containers, and we've printed the Seven Blessings (*Sheva Brachas*) in Hebrew, wrapping

❦ *OPPOSITE: Several glass containers make a clean, dramatic presentation. Each group holds a different type of flower or fruit.*

❦ *ABOVE: When the reception is held in a tent, the centerpieces should be very high to fill the empty space above.*

❦ *LEFT: Glittered oranges make a simple but beautiful centerpiece. Simply spray the unpeeled oranges with an all-purpose adhesive and roll them in glitter.*

and securing them on the outside. The candle glow lights the words from within. Use a favorite prayer, poem, or message to guests from the bride and groom.

Don't forget about table numbers, either. Use vine-wrapped, painted wooden numbers or hand-lettered, Oriental-looking calligraphy on delicate handmade paper; or paint numbers on small, oval, bone china plates. Visit your hardware store for beautiful brass numbers made for the front door, or the craft store for cut-wood numbers. Classic, gold picture frames make an easy but elegant solution to table numbers. Tiny beads can be threaded onto a thin, bendable wire and shaped into a number. Or try etching the glass of a contemporary picture frame for a clean, understated look, as shown on the opposite page.

❦ *ABOVE: Wrought-iron or brass stands are made specifically for the purpose of allowing guests to see and talk to their table-mates.*

❦ *OPPOSITE PAGE: Celebrate the words of the seventh of the* Sheva Brachot *with an autumn offering that gets the message across in a dramatic fashion. Real and faux berry branches are mixed in an urn, and the words are hung with silver threads. Try this on a sideboard or buffet.*

❦ *LEFT: White, sage green, and silver create a magical setting with the glow from long-burning, creamy tapers.*

❦ *BOTTOM: The banquet table, redefined. Low floral arrangements and scatterings of short, bright votive candles create an atmosphere of intimacy.*

Harmony
Happiness
Delight
Love
Protection
Peace
Friendship
Mr. and Mrs. Jay Freed
Ms. Sharon Berke
Mr. David Abrams

candles: a special light

❦ *ABOVE: Simple, glass hurricane globes hang from trees for a dramatic effect.*

❦ *OPPOSITE: A chunky white candle is wreathed with Nikko Blue hydrangeas for a breathtaking bouquet.*

IN JUDAISM, LIGHT HAS ALWAYS BEEN a symbol of God's presence. The light from a candle also represents the light that appeared at Mount Sinai when the Jewish people accepted the Torah given them by God. Just as there were bursts of thunder and lightning at Sinai, here the lights announce the making of a Jewish marriage. The two people escorting the bride and groom to the *chuppah* often carry braided Havdalah candles. These are the torchlike candles lit in Jewish homes on Saturday nights to signal the end of Shabbat.

Just as candle lighting on Shabbat and holidays brings both physical and spiritual light into your home, it can do the same for your wedding ceremony.

An interesting Kabbalistc interpretation is that the sum of the numerical value of the letters of the Hebrew word for candle (*ner*) multiplied by two (equaling the bride and groom) equals the sum of the letters of the Hebrew words for "be fruitful and multiply " (*Pe re ure vu*).

With this much history and symbolism surrounding light and candles, it seems that they belong in your wedding, so use them lavishly. Each place setting at your wedding dinner tables might have its own votive candle. Tucked into floral arrangements, candles have a magic of their own. Hung from trees in glass containers, they look like stars in closeup. Try floating candles in colored water, or use them in luminaries running up the aisle of the synagogue or at the entrance to the *chuppah*. We show only a few of the ways candles can light the way on your most wonderful of days.

❦ *ABOVE: Candles in glass hurricanes make a beautiful statement on the gift table. Try gel candles—made specifically for floating in water. Add a drop of food coloring to color the water for a dreamy effect.*

❦ *OPPOSITE: The soft glow of candlelight is achieved with vellum gift bags and candles sunk into colored aquarium stones. White flowers tucked into metal baskets add to the charm.*

the icing on the cake

❦ *OPPOSITE: As delicate as the paper cutwork on a wedding* ketubah, *this white-on-white fantasy cake features symmetrically placed moon, hearts, diamonds, and Jewish stars cut out from rolled fondant.*

THE CAKE AT A WEDDING IS LIKE THE curtain call in a play; but it's also a star in its own right, so make it a reflection of your personal style. Along with the couple's *ketubah,* the cake is on display for guests to admire. The cake-cutting ceremony is the last chance for the bride and groom to celebrate a time-honored ritual before the festivities are over and the guests depart. That's why the wedding cake is such a work of art—tier upon tier, flowers, fruit, luxuriant swags—hiding fillings to please the couple's individual sweet tooths. Statuesque fantasies are sliced to reveal raisin-studded carrot cakes, chocolate chip devil's food, layers of lemon or raspberry filling. Here's some cake lore:

The wedding cakes of our grandparents were often homemade and comprised one layer, reflecting the pared-down austerity of rationing during the Depression. Our mothers had many-tiered cakes, topped with the requisite generic bride and groom in miniature. Fancier weddings included entire tiny bridal parties trailing down an elaborate creation hiding a white or yellow cake inside.

Pastry chefs today treat the cake as a canvas, using airbrush techniques, a full complement of artist-caliber paintbrushes, delicate fondants, and glazing techniques. The results are the stuff of dreams, and the day's most exquisite temporary star.

Here's some wedding cake common sense, though. Keep the climate in mind, as well as the season. If yours is an outdoor wedding on a summer day, stay away from buttercream-type frosting, or your cake will look like an overemotional wedding guest. A rolled fondant is sturdier and will hold up beautifully—have a heart-to-heart talk with your pastry chef. Your cake décor should reflect the season, too. Berries, sugar acorns, and leaves make a beautiful and unique statement for an autumn wedding, and a summer cake lavished with sugared pansies or fresh flowers is a visual feast. Using real flowers (make sure they're edible) to decorate a cake is less expensive and looks beautiful.

Creating a cake with a Jewish theme can be a labor of love. The designer of the cake on the opposite page followed the theme of the couple's beautiful cut-paper *ketubah* design. She translated that simple delicacy and beauty into a four-tiered, white-on-white confection made of rolled fondant, painstaking decorated with cutouts of Jewish stars, moon, and hearts.

Don't forget about the top of the cake. A mini*chuppah* created with realistic

❦ *ABOVE: Kiddush makes the perfect themed cake for an autumn wedding.*

❦ *OPPOSITE: A popular quote and daisies make a lighthearted cake.*

marzipan ivy leaves and flowers entwined around a miniature wire garden arch is unique and distinctive. An embroidered velvet *chuppah* on traditional posts is a wonderful option, too.

Instead of one huge cake, consider several smaller ones. Some couples opt for one cake per each table; these can take the place of a centerpiece. Tiny individual cakes for each place setting are a charming addition and act a favors, too. It's up to you to make a lasting statement with your cake—a spectacular, if short-lived, star at your wedding.

I am my
my beloved is mine
is mine I am my
my beloved's and my

wedding day mitzvahs

❦ *OPPOSITE: Consider donating your wedding dress to an agency that helps outfit poor or orphaned Jewish brides.*

❦ *ABOVE: An unusual but heartfelt centerpiece idea —miniature shopping carts filled with canned goods and a note explaining that in lieu of floral centerpieces, the food will be donated to a food pantry.*

CHESED HAS ALWAYS BEEN CONSIDERED an important part of Jewish life, and it means acting with kindness and generosity. It is considered a special mitzvah to perform acts of *chesed* on one's wedding day.

In Hasidic neighborhoods all over New York, it is a custom to set extra tables for the poor or homeless, and all, whether known or strangers, are welcome to join the wedding dinner for a hearty meal and the joy of the *simcha.*

A wedding, as Rabbi Eliyahu Dressler once said, should signal a life of giving, not taking, and it is fitting that this chord be struck at the very beginning of the marriage. Here are some ways for you to perform mitzvot on the occasion of your wedding.

Consider donating your wedding gown to a Jewish agency that provides wedding finery to poor brides, both in Israel and here in the United States. Before you send a gown to a particular agency, check to see if there are any *tzinus,* or modesty, restrictions that may include sleeve length, necklines, and backs.

If any parents of either the bride or groom are deceased, it is customary to visit the grave site and recite Kaddish, or memorial prayer. If the grave sites are many states away, contributing to charity in memory of the deceased parent is a worthy alternative.

You may want to give 10 percent of the money you receive as gifts to your favorite charity. Or ask your caterer to pack up all the wedding's leftovers and have someone bring them to a local soup kitchen.

Flowers from the ceremony can be brought to a retirement home or hospital, so that the bouquets can brighten the day for others.

See "Wedding Day Mitzvahs" in the Resource Guide for a listing of charities.

For the sake of my love, place me like a seal on Your heart, like a seal to dedicate Your strength for me. ~*Song of Songs 8:6*

CHAPTER FOUR

REAL JEWISH weddings

JEWISH WEDDINGS ARE AS VARIED AS SNOWFLAKES, NOT the stereotypical old vision of chopped liver mounds and ice molds. In this chapter we're giving you a glimpse into some real Jewish weddings, from Caracas, Venezuela, to Seattle, Washington, with real-live brides and grooms. Meet Robyn and Jared, who married in a classic New York City style; Dana and Jacob, a Sephardic couple who married in Venezuela with more than a thousand guests; Jackie and Bennett, who chose an outdoor wedding in lovely San Diego, California; Chana and Shalom, a Lubavitch couple who married in true Hasidic tradition in Hartford, Connecticut; Esther and Andrew, who married in his mother's lush garden in Seattle, Washington; Lori and Michael, who loved the glamorous backdrop of Palm Beach, Florida; and Leslie and Mark, who celebrated their love in quiet Bedford Corners, New York, in the crisp autumn air.

These couples and their wedding styles may seem radically different, but they have more in common than you think. From the henna-painted bride from Venezuela to the Hasidic wedding with more guests than there are residents in some small towns, to the casual outdoor garden wedding—each couple wanted a Jewish wedding.

So take a peek into their wedding days. You might want to borrow a few of their ideas and mix them with your own to create your own unique wedding.

New York, New York

Robyn Finkelstein and Jared Fischer

THANKS TO HER YEARS OF STUDYING dance, Robyn Finkelstein's wedding to Jared Fischer was executed with the drama and excitement of *Swan Lake,* right down to the palest pink accents on her dress and the ivory on her bridesmaids'. Abundant fresh flowers were everywhere. The classical, austere beauty of a private club in midtown Manhattan was the jewel in the setting—the perfect ambiance for a formal, yet festively joyous occasion.

Being surrounded by a loving clan of family and friends on the days leading to the wedding made it even more wonderful. The eve of the wedding turned into a giant pajama party. Robyn, her bridesmaids, and her mom slept at the club, each clad in silky matching robes—the ultimate party favor.

Both the Finkelstein and Fischer families are from Westchester County, New York, just a short drive from the city. The year both families independently decided

❦ *ABOVE: The view from Fifth Avenue looking south, just around the corner from the private club where Robyn and Jared's wedding took place.*

❦ *OPPOSITE: The new couple are all smiles after their wedding ceremony.*

to vacation on Antigua, Robyn was a student at the University of Michigan and Jared was studying at the University of Miami. Through mutual friends, Robyn and Jared were introduced, and they became inseparable—it was love at first sight.

Five years later, they became engaged. Robyn and her parents knew that they wanted a beautiful wedding in the most exciting city in the world, and Dr. Finkelstein, an obstetrician-gynecologist with a practice in New York, carefully collected tips on florists, caterers, and perfect settings from his many patients.

The result was elegant, yet fun—and Robyn's personality shone through on her special day. A "take the cake" story: Robyn and her mom sampled their way through New York City in search of the perfect wedding cake, but the bride decided what she really wanted was a cake she grew up with—a Duncan Hines chocolate cake, made moist with pistachio pudding and studded liberally with chocolate chips! To appease the pastry chef, they split up and scoured just about every grocery store in New York for dozens of little boxes of now hard-to-find instant pistachio pudding!

Gifts for the bridesmaids were chosen with love and caring, too. In addition to their silk party robes, each received a sterling silver, purse-sized perfume bottle. The men in the wedding party received silver lighters from a tobacconist. Innovative bow ties were gifts of choice for the men as well.

❦ *RIGHT: The dining room—replete with topiary and crystal—is ready for guests to enter.*

❦ *CLOCKWISE FROM TOP LEFT: Robyn surround by her bridesmaids, Amy Gallatin, Sara Kleban, Jennifer Fischer, Emily Nadler, and Alissa Mark; a very special* ketubah; *Robyn's parents, Patricia and Joseph Finkelstein, beam on the joyous occasion; who would ever guess that Duncan Hines was invited to the festivities, hidden by the elegant draped fondant cake; the night-before pajama party with all the girls relaxing in their matching robes.*

❦ *OPPOSITE: Simple white votives transform a plain hallway.*

❦ *CLOCKWISE FROM TOP LEFT: Purse-sized silver perfume bottles with tiny funnels for pouring were elegant and beautiful gifts for the bridesmaids; the first dance; a simple yet elegant engraved invitation set the mood for this graceful affair; a sushi station was just one of many hors d' oeuvres offerings at the reception; place cards are arranged under a pedestal festooned with silky flowers.*

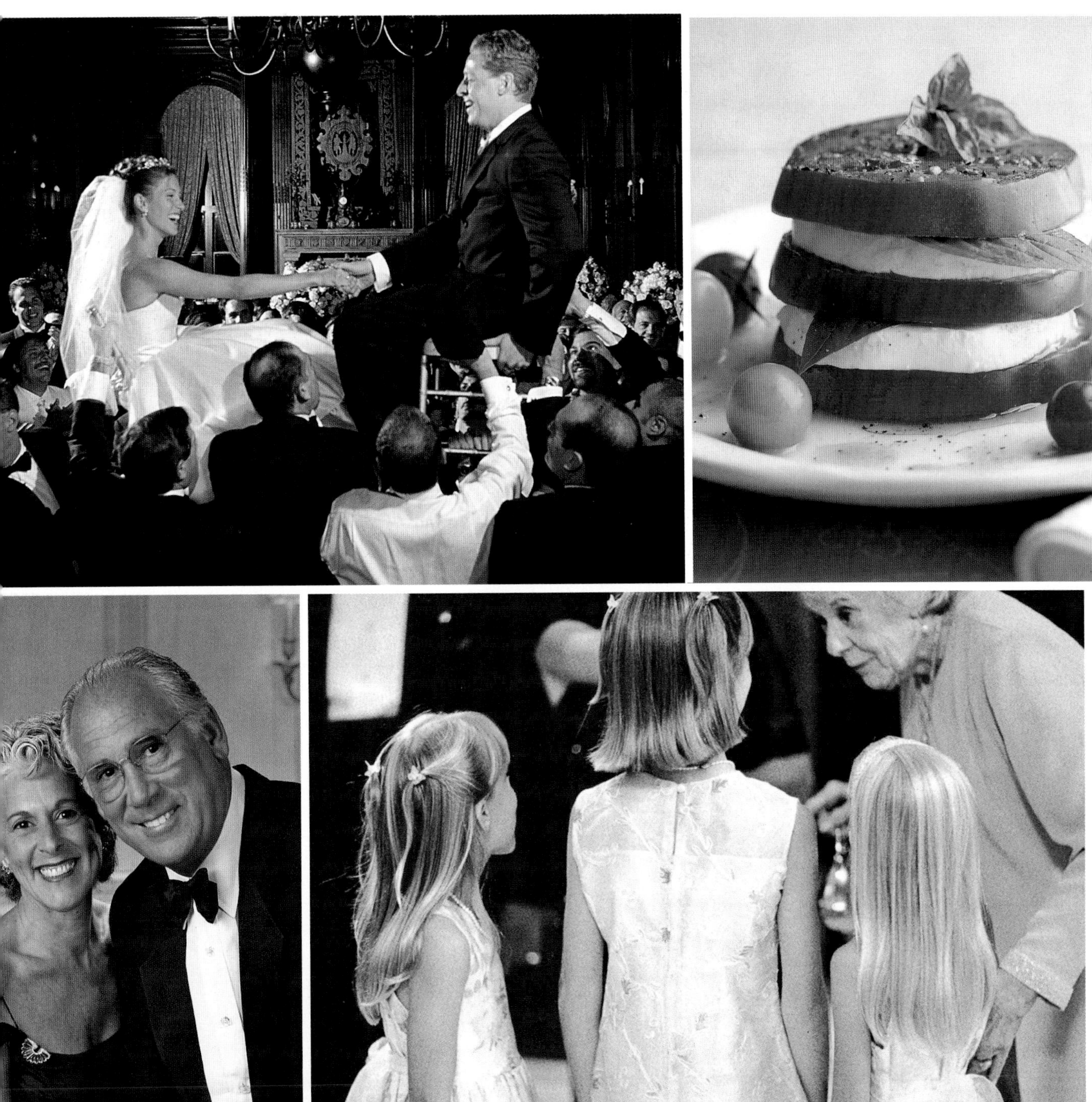

❦ *CLOCKWISE FROM TOP LEFT: In keeping with Jewish tradition, the couple is lifted on chairs for a dance together; a colorful, stacked mozzarella-and-tomato salad sat in for a leafy green salad; a trio of Jared's young cousins, Danielle, Chelsea, and Nicole Adler get some advice from their grandmother Beryl Adler; Jared's parents, Susan and Douglas Fischer, smile for the camera.*

Caracas, Venezuela

Dana Guenoun and Jacob Tangir

❦ *ABOVE: A heavy gold-printed card on each table explained the henna ceremony in detail on the evening of the* berberisca, *or henna night.*

❦ *OPPOSITE: Dana's traditional Jewish Moroccan attire included an ornamental crown with long detachable braids; long, jewel-encrusted earrings; and traditional heavy eye makeup.*

FOR MOST OF US, IT'S DAUNTING enough to juggle the logistics of just one wedding, but imagine having to have three separate celebrations, all in the space of a few weeks. Not tiny affairs, either—two had 250 guests, and the other had 800!

Such was the case of Dana (pronounced "Donna") Guenoun and her fiancé, Jacob Tangir, both of Caracas, Venezuela. The tightly knit Jewish population of Caracas is one in which everyone goes to the same day schools, Jewish high schools, organizations, clubs, vacations spots, and social occasions. So when there's a wedding, everyone is invited. In fact, although Jacob is three years older than Dana, they met and fell in love at a high school reunion when both were on the planning committee.

Dana was born in Israel and moved to Venezuela as a small child, and so did Jacob, except that his family moved to Caracas from Morocco. So when the marriage was announced, it was understood that there would be three ceremonies, following the traditions of the families.

The first marriage was a civil ceremony that took place a month before the wedding, and is required by Venezuelan law. This was no city hall affair, either—this ceremony was attended by 250 guests and was complete with music, dancing, photographers, and a sit-down dinner.

The second ceremony was the henna night (called in Spanish *berberisca*), a common practice for Sephardic Jews, which took place the Wednesday before the Jewish wedding.

During the month between the civil ceremony and the henna night, every weekend was packed with dinners, parties, *aufrufs,* and even a *mikvah* party for Dana, given by her sister.

❦ *CLOCKWISE FROM TOP LEFT: Dana and Jacob enjoy the henna ceremony; a Moroccan-style blend of couscous, raisins, squash, and almonds was served with chicken with green olives; Dana is being dressed for the ceremony by a cousin, Patricia Cohen, and her daughter, Natalie; the bride's palms, and those of every female guest in attendance, were painted with henna; local nuts and dried fruits were placed on every table; the mother-in-law officially welcomes her new daughter-in-law with a glass of water and candy so that her life will be pure and sweet, according to tradition.*

The henna ceremony is both magnificent and regal. The bride and her attendants have their hands painted with henna, a temporary vegetable dye, believed to bring good luck. The bride is dressed in traditional garb, handed down through the generations, called *keswa el kbira,* made of velvet and heavy silk embroidery, with a lavish headpiece, heavy makeup, special jewelry, and even a long braided hairpiece. The process of simply getting ready for the ceremony is so intricate that dressers are called in to help—for Dana, her cousin Patricia Cohen. These experts also heap blessings on the bride and direct traditional wedding songs. They supervise the henna painting and draw a *hamsa,* or hand, on the door of the house to guard against evil spirits. The ceremonial outfits, according to custom, are usually green or blue for women in the interior cities, garnet red for families who live in the coastal cities.

Let's take a closer look at this ceremony, because it is so fascinating: While the bride is being dressed, the groom is praying with a minyan. Later, the bride receives a stomp on the foot (gently we assume) as a sign, some say, of his dominance and her submission, to which she responds with a stomp of her own! The bride then sits in a high, thronelike

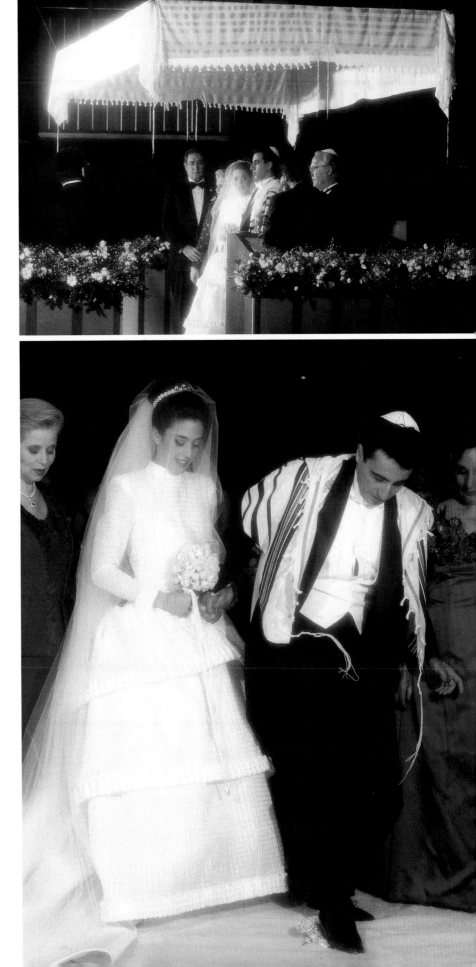

❦ *TOP RIGHT: The* chuppah *is suspended from the ceiling with string instead of being supported by poles.*

❦ *BOTTOM RIGHT: Jacob crushes the glass with his foot, symbolizing the destruction of the second temple. Both mothers, Gisela Guenoun and Alegria Tangir, are close at hand.*

chair with velvet decorations and padding that is similar to a Torah covering to receive the blessings of her guests. The significance of the regal chair covering is to highlight the important role of the Jewish woman.

The Jewish wedding ceremony took place on the following Sunday evening, with eight hundred guests filling the Caracas synagogue. Afterward, the dancing was high-spirited and joyous, and guests partied to the illumination of thousands of white twinkle lights tucked among the ficus trees lining the huge room.

Finally, after three *simchas* and thirteen hundred guests, a very happy and very exhausted Dana and Jacob escaped the mob and left for their honeymoon in California.

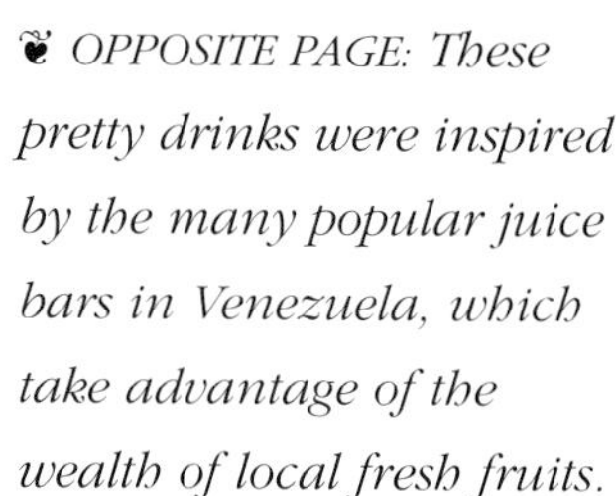

❦ *OPPOSITE PAGE: These pretty drinks were inspired by the many popular juice bars in Venezuela, which take advantage of the wealth of local fresh fruits.*

❦ *CLOCKWISE FROM TOP LEFT: Wedding favors were pastel Jordan almonds in clear plastic boxes, tied with a Sephardic* hamsa *charm, said to ward off the evil eye; Dana poses with her flower girl and her eight attendants; candlelight gives light to your marriage, and these candles are nestled in silk leaves laced with tiny white lights; Jacob is lifted high in a celebratory dance; a profile portrait shows Dana with her bouquet.*

San Diego, California

Jacqueline Sherman and Bennett Gross

After more than a year of eating at the same Chinese restaurant Jackie finally got a fortune
Sherman and Bennett Gross will be married on
OCTOBER 31,
California and more information will be coming shortly on hotels
weekend. We are looking forward to celebrating with you!
Save the date!
Jackie + Bennett
You or a close friend will be married within a year.

❦ *ABOVE: Save-the-date cards, designed by Jackie, with a theme inspired by her all-time favorite fortune cookie.*

SOMETIMES THINGS DON'T HAPPEN exactly as you plan. The reservations were made, the ring was chosen, and Bennett was still working on the most exciting part—the proposal.

Then the phone rang with the message from the jewelry store: the ring was ready, but somehow incredibly given to the wrong person—Jackie.

Feeling excited it finally happened, but at the same time a little deflated at the turn of events, the now-engaged couple decided to go to their favorite Chinese restaurant to celebrate. After the meal was over, there was still one more surprise—for of all the fortune cookies Jackie had ever opened, she had never found a fortune like this: "You or a close friend will be married within a year." But then again, Jackie had never been engaged before.

Jackie is a graphic designer with her own business, specializing in invitations, unique stationery and thank-you notes, so designing these witty save-the-date cards was a natural for her.

The couple originally met as students at the University of Pennsylvania in Philadelphia. They met again through mutual friends when Bennett moved to California, and they realized that this was no accident. They had found each other, this time for good. They were *barshert.*

Jackie and Bennett decided, for the sake of sanity, to put their wedding together in just six months. After all, as Jackie says with a laugh, "Any more time than that, and my mother and I would have gone crazy!" Most of the planning and execution was done by Jackie, her mom,

Barbara Sherman, and a few close friends.

The Four Seasons Aviara in Carlsbad , California, was chosen as the wedding site, because of its perfect combination of a lovely outdoor atmosphere for the ceremony and spacious, lovely indoor facilities for their reception and dinner.

The couple incorporated several beautiful, ancient Jewish traditions into their special day. Bennett had an *aufruf* in synagogue before the wedding; he was pelted with candies and there were cries of *"Mazel tov!"* in his honor. They also decided on the ancient custom of *yichud*—a quiet time alone after the wedding and before the party. Their wedding took place on October 31—always Halloween in America—which set the scene for another comedic glitch. Running down the hall hand in hand after the ceremony to their suite, they realized they had no key and needed a bellhop with a master key. After taking a long look at the bride and groom, the bellhop thought they were just another crazy couple in Halloween costumes and refused to open their door until he realized that they were indeed newlyweds! Inside, they found a chilled bottle of champagne and a snack—especially welcome since neither had eaten much that day.

Extra touches made this wedding special, not just for the bridal couple, but for the guests as well. Out-of-town guests found thoughtful wedding bags filled with edibles in their rooms; a fragrant rose rested on every napkin at dinner; and as a nod to the Halloween festivities taking place in the outside world, baskets of candy corn were passed around on the transport bus from the wedding back to the guests' hotels.

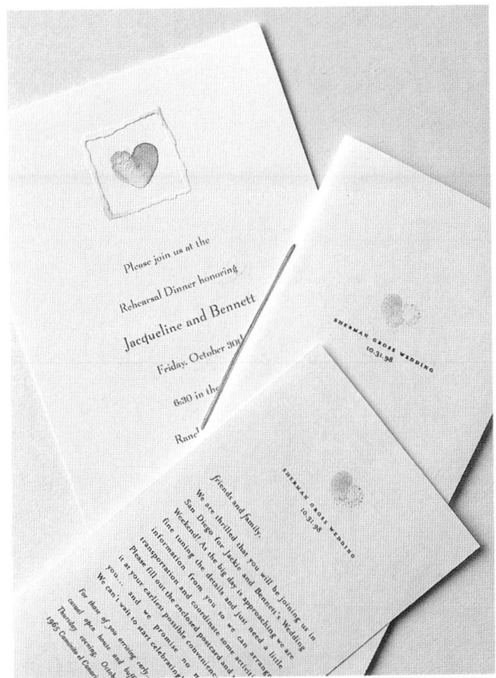

❦ *CLOCKWISE FROM TOP LEFT: Jackie used their two thumbprints to form a heart on mailings; Jackie posed with her bridesmaids, Kappy Sugawara, Debbie Glazer, Michelle Gross, and Marian Sherman; Bennett smiles with his happy parents, Ronald and Grecia Gross; handmade paper bags were filled with food treats and waited for out-of-town guests; flowers for the bridesmaids stay fresh before the wedding.*

❦ *OPPOSITE TOP: A* chuppah *is festooned with flowers as another Jewish family is created.*

❦ *OPPOSITE BOTTOM: Guests heft chairs high holding the bride and groom in joyous celebratory dancing.*

❦ *CLOCKWISE FROM TOP LEFT: The wedding cake is decorated with a garden of pale roses; Jackie poses with her parents, Barbara and Lawrence Sherman; a serious moment before the ceremony—the signing of the* ketubah; *paper cones, embellished with calligraphy in gold ink and created by Jackie's friend, Leslie Simon, hold fragrant rose petals; the new Dr. and Mrs. Gross beam a pair of thousand-watt smiles.*

❦ *OPPOSITE: Dinner tables glow with candlelight, creamy white roses and green hydrangea. Each place setting has a rose tucked into the napkin tied with a sheer brown ribbon.*

Hartford, Connecticut

Chana Gopin and Shalom Lew

EXACTLY FOUR WEEKS AND SEVEN dates after meeting for the first time, Chana Gopin of Hartford, Connecticut, and Shalom Lew, of London, became engaged. Three months later, they were married in a traditional Hasidic wedding with over five hundred jubilant guests. Sound like a whirlwind courtship? Actually, among a group of Jews called the Lubavitch, it is the norm. And, as far as the planning goes, the preparations can be compared to Inauguration Day and the presidential parade down Pennsylvania Avenue.

Although the Lubavitch Hasidim have a presence around the globe, their network is tight, and friends and families are always on the lookout for a *shiddach*, or match.

As it turned out, Chana's *barshert* was right in Crown Heights, Brooklyn, studying in Yeshiva to be a rabbi. Chana went to high school in Crown Heights and has many relatives and friends in this enclave, well known as the official headquarters for Lubavitch Jews, and home for over half a century of perhaps the most widely known rabbi in modern history—Menachem Mendel Schneerson, the seventh Lubavitch leader, who was known affectionately simply as "the rebbe."

❦ *LEFT: Male relatives and friends—a sea of black hats—surround the groom, clapping and singing as they escort the groom to the* chuppah.

❦ *RIGHT: Chana gets a loving hug from her grandfather, who made the long journey from Australia to attend her wedding.*

❦ *OPPOSITE CLOCKWISE FROM TOP LEFT: Chana and Rabbi Lew smile for their formal wedding portrait; prayer books, called* benchers, *are imprinted with the couple's names and wedding date (these booklets are at each place setting and will be used for after-meal prayers); the unveiling ceremony, a tradition that hails back to the times of Leah and Rachel, was meant to reassure the groom that he was marrying the right bride; the party room, elegantly dressed in fresh white linen, awaits the guests, with men and women seated separately.*

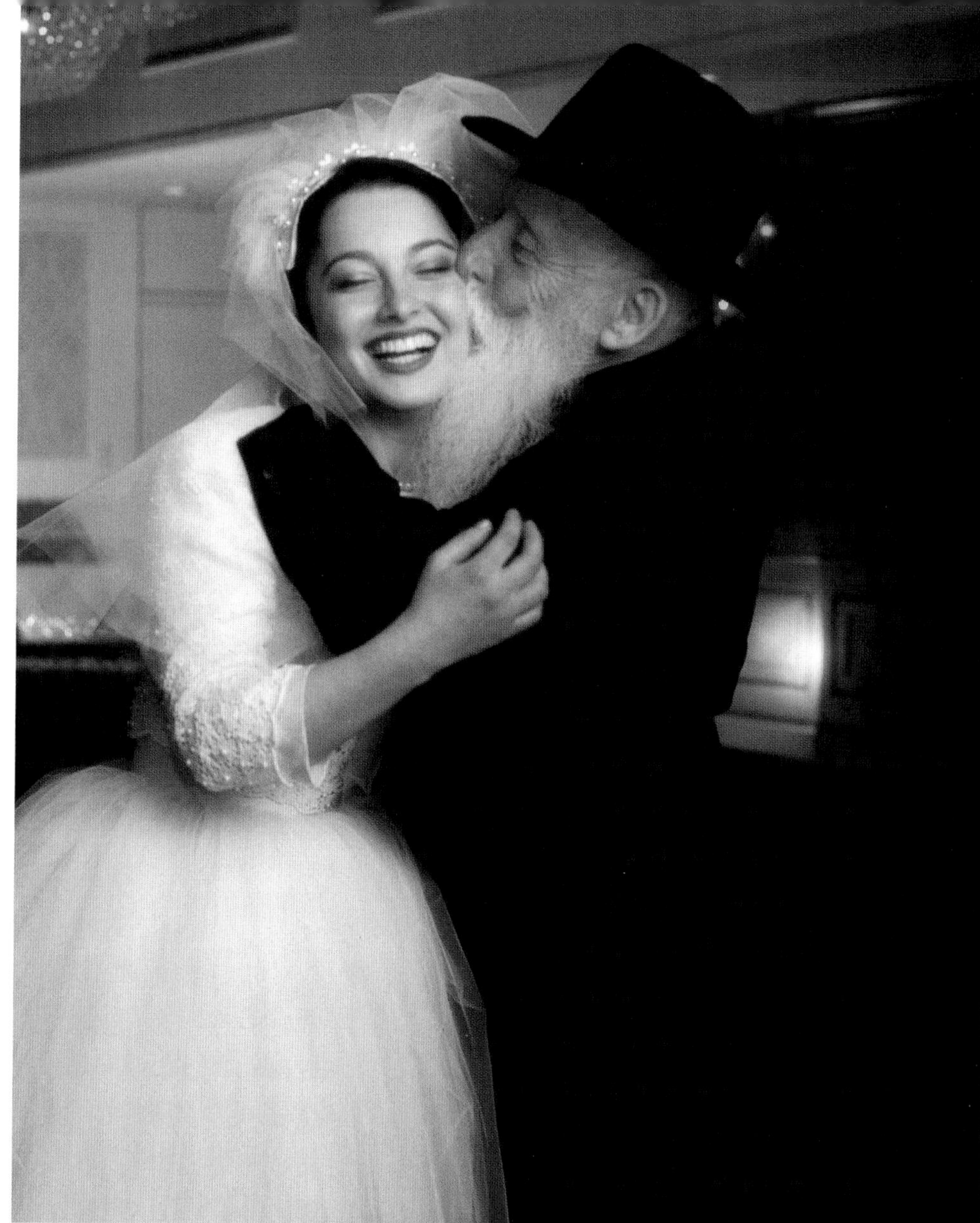

Long before the first meeting took place, there was a seemingly endless flurry of phone calls, faxes, and interviews—from Chana's parents to Shalom's, to his friends, fellow students, teachers, and even the head of his yeshiva—all to make certain that this would be a blissful match. To explain the intense scrutiny, Lubavitch Jews do not date until they are ready to marry, and the goal of dating is to find one's spouse. Many people are asked to be character witnesses for both parties, again to ensure a perfect *shiddach*.

When the go-ahead came through, Shalom and Chana finally spoke on the phone and made a date to meet at her parents' home in West Hartford, Connecticut. On the appointed day, at the agreed-upon time, Shalom was nowhere in sight. Chana was getting a bit nervous, until he called on his cell phone to let her know that his car had overheated an exit away. So Chana hopped into her car to find him, and ended up meeting her future husband on the shoulder of a busy highway.

Rabbi Lew explains, "Before we met, we were already seventy percent of the way there. After we met, it didn't take us

very long to realize the other thirty percent was also there."

Marriage is important to the Lubavitch sect, named after a small town in Poland where the movement was begun less than two hundred years ago by the group's first leader, or rebbe—the revered Shneur Zalman. His objective was to revitalize the oppressed Jews of Eastern Europe with a decidedly spirited return to Judaism and God. Having celebrations, marriages, many children and generations of family to sing, dance, and worship Judaism joyfully was, and still is, a primary goal of the Lubavitch.

Chana and Shalom's wedding was a joyous one, not limited to family and friends, but involving the entire community as well. The *chuppah* took place outdoors, at night, under the stars, in traditional Hasidic manner. Before the *chuppah,* Shalom was entertained by his friends and even a professional juggler, as *"L'Chaim"* toasts were passed his way. Chana sat like a princess on a thronelike rattan peacock chair, surrounded by her

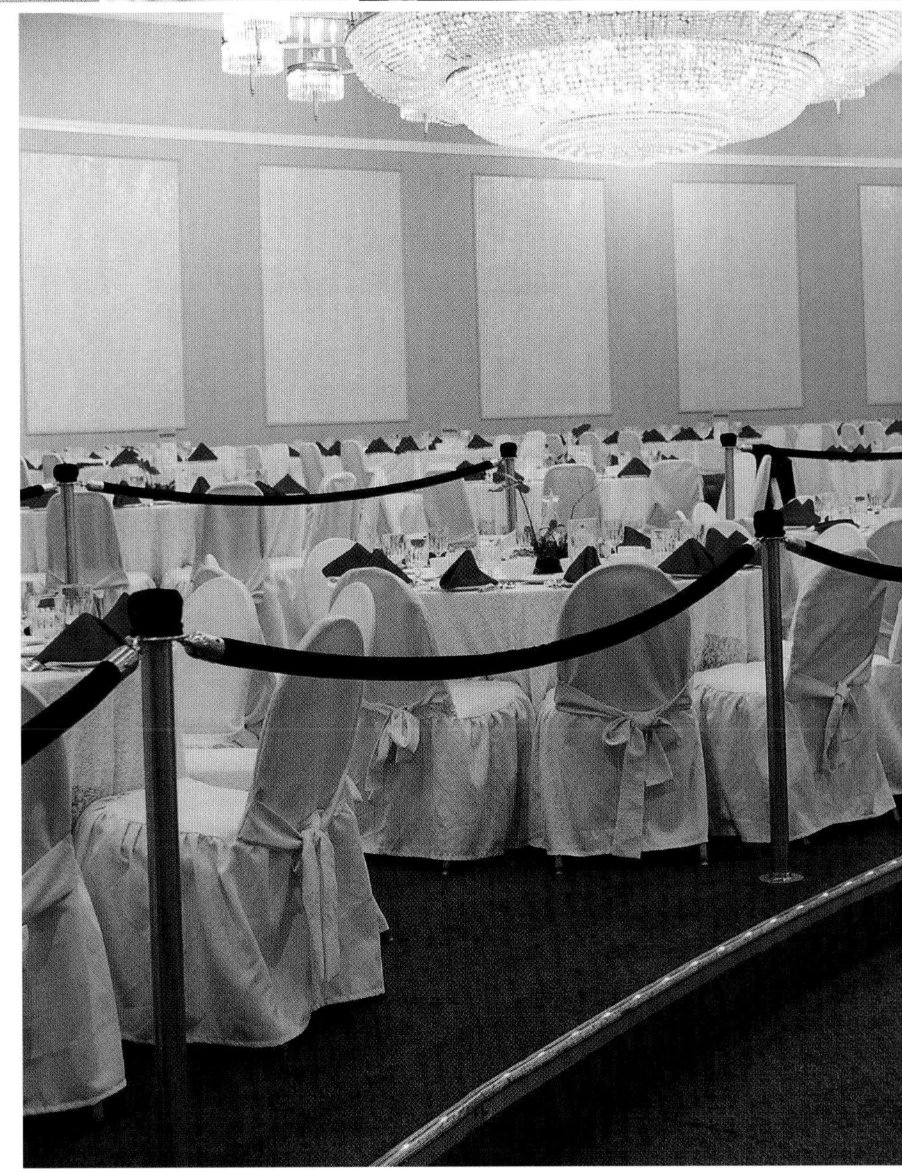

❦ *ABOVE TOP: Sabra, the Israeli-made liqueur, is served on each table.*

❦ *ABOVE: A fire-throwing juggler entertains the groom much the way it was done years ago.*

❦ *OPPOSITE: The photographer captures Chana and her brother Dovie in an endearing portrait.*

female family and friends, receiving female well-wishers. The meal was a hearty, delicious, and traditional one: matzoh ball soup, meats, roasted chicken, kugels, and fanciful desserts.

The Lews had already decided on a career path—together. After the devastation of the Holocaust, the rebbe escaped to New York with a few hundred followers. He sent young married couples to far-flung areas, not just in America, but all over the world, to rekindle the Jewish spirit, by opening centers called Chabad Houses. These brave couples, called *shluchim* (messengers), leave their large families, often for the first time, to go to areas that often lack kosher food, religious schools for their children, and the company of other Lubavitch. These are not temporary assignments—the couples go with the intention of staying permanently. Couples like Chana and Shalom have opened more than three thousand such Chabad Houses, from Las Vegas, Nevada, to Nepal and Russia.

Chana and Shalom were carefully trained for their roles as Chabad House pioneers, and the post they chose for themselves was in Glendale, Arizona.

As Chana says, "Every Jew is important. Frankly, it's easy for me to do a mitzvah, because I was born into it. My parents founded a Chabad House, and we all grew up as children of *shluchim*. But when a Jew lights Shabbat candles for the very first time, that's when God is really pleased."

Rabbi Lew adds, "It is our job to teach others about Judaism. It doesn't matter to us if you think of yourself as Reform, Conservative, Orthodox, or unaffiliated. Because for us, if you're Jewish you're Jewish; it's intrinsic and those are only labels. Our Chabad Houses, unlike synagogues, have no membership fees or dues. We teach classes, and what you do with what you learn—well, that's up to you. We want people to come and learn, or come for a festive Shabbat meal; there's lots of singing and good company."

If you ever get down to Glendale, stop by and visit this very special couple, and be prepared to spend an unforgettable Shabbat with Chana and Shalom Lew.

Seattle, Washington

Esther Gehrman and Andrew Sirotnik

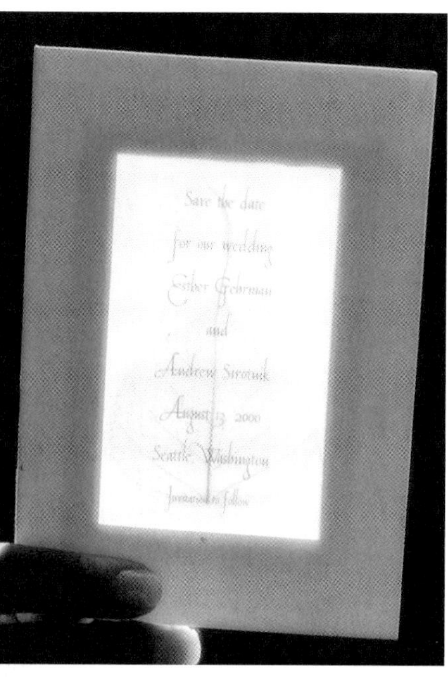

❦ *ABOVE: In tune with nature, save-the-date cards bear the fragile strength of a simple leaf motif.*

SUDDEN RAINSTORMS. BLIZZARDS. A bolt of lightning. When it comes to matchmaking sometimes even the forces of nature can play a role, and Esther and Andrew's story can reinforce this theory, with the tale of their wintry meeting.

Although Esther went to high school on Mercer Island, Washington, with Matthew Sirotnik, she had never met his big brother Andrew, who was living in Berkeley, California. A few years after graduation, Esther called Matthew to get together during winter break, but since he was waiting for his brother to fly in for a visit, he invited Esther to join them with a group of their friends. Andrew's plane was late because of snow, but when it finally arrived, he ended up missing his return flight, calling his office to say he was "snowed in"—with Esther! Happy ending: They dated long distance for eighteen months until Esther graduated from law school and could join Andrew in California.

A creative and energetic couple, Andrew is a founder and director of Creative Services at the San Francisco media firm Fluid, and Esther practices law in Oakland.

Small wonder, then, that they knew exactly how they wanted their wedding

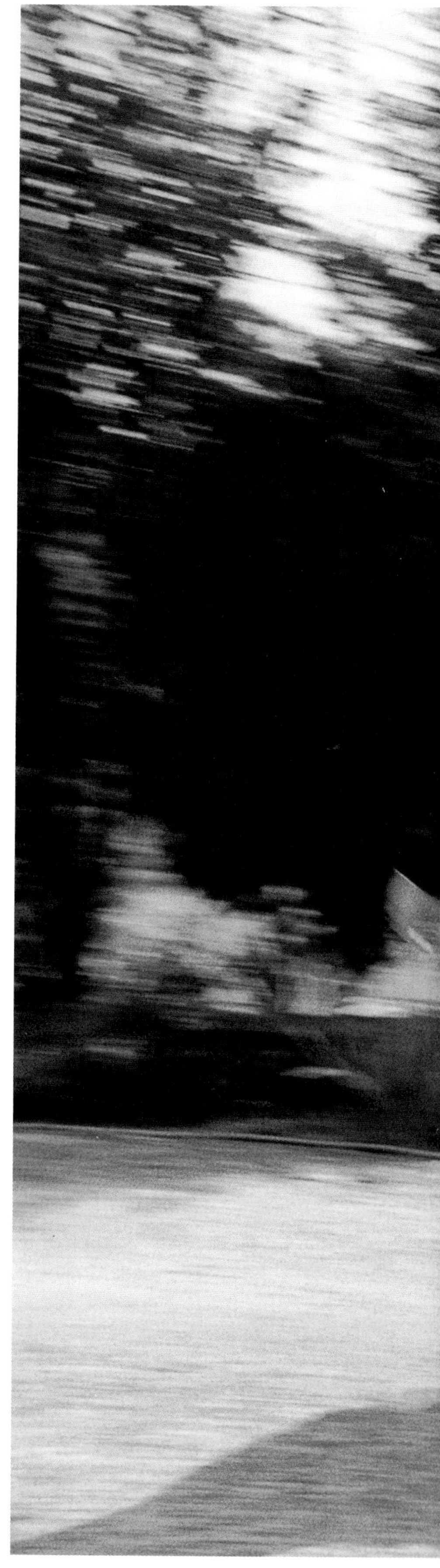

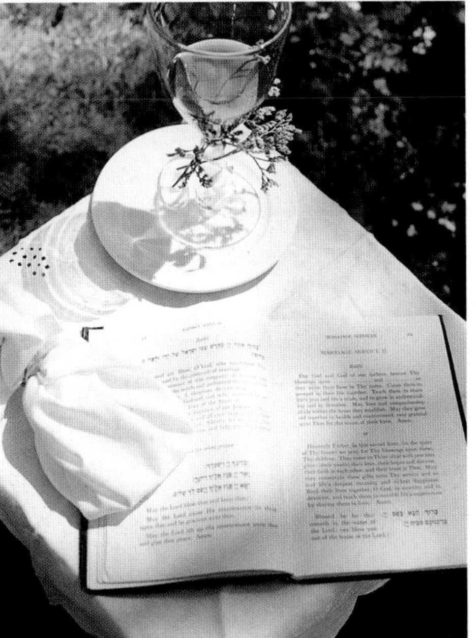

to be, and nature played a hand in the decorations, too. Andrew's mom, Sheryl Sirotnik is a landscape architect, and her Kirkland, Washington, garden is lush and elegant. As soon as the couple announced plans to have the wedding at the groom's mother's home, she started plantings that were timed to bloom around the wedding date. The wedding took place in the garden, which created a relaxed and colorful mood for the ceremony and party to follow. More family

❦ *CLOCKWISE FROM TOP LEFT: Andrew and Esther equals joy and laughter—a happy equation; custom-compiled jazz CDs made lasting party favors, and guests got a preview of the music during the cocktail hour; Esther's mom, Sandra Gehrman, blows a bubble tribute after the ceremony; the wineglass ready to be crushed under Andrew's foot; velvety and deep—Esther's unusual bouquet featured a rich collage of deep burgundy roses and calla lilies.*

❦ *OPPOSITE: Rabbi Theodore Stainman conducts the service under a simple white* chuppah.

and friends got into the planning spirit as well, since Esther and Andrew were living in California. Although they took frequent hops to Washington to interview caterers, photographers and musicians, Andrew's brother Matthew served as event coordinator. A family friend, B. J. Livingston, designed the name cards for the table seating, designed flowers for the guest chairs, and arranged fresh bouquets of homegrown flowers for the cocktail hour.

The couple even compiled their own jazz CD, which played in the background during the cocktail reception after the ceremony and before the meal. Copies of the CD were party favors for each guest to take home.

They were married in a ceremony under a simple white *chuppah* that swayed gently in the breeze—held aloft by four close friends. A beautiful wedding—West Coast style.

❦ *CLOCKWISE FROM TOP LEFT: Andrew shares a happy moment with his dad, Ken Sirotnik; together for the first time, Esther and Andrew share a moment after the ceremony; the clean look of simple white folding chairs are garnished with fresh bouquets from the surrounding gardens and rose petals are scattered on the ground.*

❦ *OPPOSITE: Pastel calla lilies for the bridal party, pinned in preparation, are ready to go.*

Palm Beach, Florida

Lori Weitzman and Michael Bernstein

TIMING IS EVERYTHING. LORI AND Michael met each other time and again over the course of several years while both their families vacationed in Palm Beach. Their paths also briefly crossed while Michael, a business major at Georgetown University, was visiting friends at the University of Pennsylvania—coincidently, the same school where Lori was majoring in communications.

Typically, at each encounter, Michael would ask Lori for her telephone number but would never call her. There was even an occasion during Lori's senior year at Penn when a mutual friend attempted to set the two up. Lori laughed at the idea and said, "Sure, you can give Michael my number, but he'll never call!" Sure enough, he didn't. Life went on.

Finally, though neither was aware of it, after graduation, each moved to Palm Beach. After one year of living under the same sunny skies, their paths crossed again. Only this time, the timing was just right. When they ran into each other this time, they engaged in a long conversation, learning that they shared a love for tennis and much more. That evening they arranged a tennis date for the following day. Knowing Michael's previous track record, Lori called him the next morning and the rest was history. About one year later, on the Fourth of July, Lori and Michael became engaged in Rome and made plans to get married the following spring.

Lori and Michael decided to have a wedding similar to the one Lori's parents had had when they got married—a small, intimate wedding ceremony consisting mostly of immediate family and a few very close friends, followed by a larger reception a few days later.

Since Lori's mom is her best friend, Lori wanted to share her experience and honor her mom by wearing her 1960s street-length wedding dress with its matching fur-trimmed jacket, adorned with a pin of her grandmother's on the pocket.

The couple chose Mar-a-Lago in Palm Beach for the wedding ceremony and for the reception two days later. The elegant supper following the ceremony for the newlyweds and their twenty-eight guests was served in the club's private dining room with open-air arches and breathtaking views of manicured grounds and the Intercoastal Waterway.

The reception, two nights later, coincided with April Fool's Day. It was created by Bruce Sutka, a well-known Palm Beach party planner. He created a magical Palm Beach winter wonderland by designing a tent that remarkably resembled a

❦ *The majestic beauty of Palm Beach makes the perfect setting for a south Florida wedding.*

3 FT 6 IN

❦ *CLOCKWISE FROM TOP LEFT: The couple married under a* chuppah *of lace and ivy; Michael was escorted down the aisle by his two beautiful mothers, Carol Weitzman and Susan Bernstein; gator cookies were iced and decorated by Lori for out-of-town guests; a solemn moment for Lori and Michael was the veiling ceremony.*

snow globe—an April Fool's surprise. And, to the delight of the guests, "snow" even fell from the "sky" during the first dance. Dancers dressed as swans and snowflakes even escorted guests to their tables! Silvery leaves were scattered about each table, and the centerpieces were five-foot potted gold palm trees interwoven with white Dendrobium orchids, and lilies painted silver and gold. The atmosphere was truly magical—a perfect backdrop for a wedding celebration.

The elegance and imagination for this

special wedding was created with lots of input from Lori and her mother, reflecting their love of Palm Beach and their delight in detail. Lori even baked alligator cookies as Florida souvenirs for the out-of-town guests' hotel goodie bags.

As a thoughtful tribute, Lori's and Michael's parents were presented with a special gift from the couple at the reception: Lovely sterling silver plates that bore the engraved word, "Mom and Dad, You mean the world to us." These special gifts fit in with the mitzvah of honoring one's parents on the wedding day.

❦ *ABOVE: A special dinner followed the wedding ceremony. Each place setting featured an orchid inscribed with the guest's name for place-setting favors.*

❦ *LEFT: Colorful pashmina shawls were worn by the bridesmaids, Candee Weitzman, Lisa Weitzman, and Sara Bernstein-Handreke.*

Mr. Michael Bernstein
Mr. and Mrs. Michael Bernstein

❦ *OPPOSITE CLOCKWISE FROM TOP: The cocktail reception at poolside glows at night; an assortment of silvery frames with "Tiffany blue" place cards marked each guest's place—calligraphy was used on all the pieces for a consistent look; Lori and Michael pose with pet pooch Bellini, who was also invited to the cocktail hour; beautiful place settings featured Lori's handmade silk flowers on each woman's plate and, tucked into the folds of each male guest's napkin, a chocolate heart wrapped in gold foil.*

❦ *ABOVE: The reception tent was disguised as a winter wonderland, complete with snowflakes, lights, and gold and silver palm trees.*

Bedford Corners, New York

Leslie Caney and Mark Berni

❦ *ABOVE: Even a sprinkle couldn't dampen the spirits of the bride, Leslie Caney Berni, followed by her sister, Elizabeth Caney; mom, Emily Caney; and sister-in-law, Lynn Berni.*

❦ *OPPOSITE Leslie's and Mark's names are calligraphed on wide ribbon and pinned to a pumpkin—used generously throughout the reception.*

SOMETIMES LOVE IS RIGHT AROUND the corner—just ask Leslie Caney and Mark Berni. Leslie and Mark were high school friends in Stamford, Connecticut, and their friendship continued when they attended the University of Vermont.

After college, though, they went their separate ways. Leslie went to New York to pursue a publishing career. Mark headed out west to ski for a few years before getting settled with a serious job. After seven long years and a few jobs around the country, Leslie moved back up north. She heard Mark was in town and then had a dream about him, so she called him the next morning. Before long, they picked up right where they had left off—at first.

They loved their jobs—Leslie as founding editor for *Fairfield County Magazine*, a new regional publication, and Mark, working as a trader for a private hedge fund. They loved the breathtaking surroundings of rural Fairfield County, too—taking long walks along country roads, and enjoying the beauty of the changing seasons. And just around the time when the dogwood came into

Leslie and Mark

❦ *ABOVE: Temple Shaaray Tefila, once a recital hall on the Baldwin estate in Bedford Corners, was an elegant setting for the ceremony.*

bloom, they realized that love had blossomed for them as well—this time, they knew they were more than friends. An engagement quickly followed, and the wedding was planned for eight months later.

Large wedding halls with multiple parties going on at once were not their style; when they discovered Temple Shaaray Tefila in Bedford Corners, New York, just a short drive from Connecticut, they immediately knew they had found a special place.

Set at the end of a winding country road, the temple is hidden in the woods on the site of the old Baldwin estate. It was occasionally used as a recital hall and made for a beautiful setting for the ceremony. Across a circular driveway from the temple sits a pretty mansion—now used as a reception hall, with a kosher kitchen.

Leslie and Mark asked their favorite club band to play at their wedding and worked closely with a New Jersey–based caterer to serve food that fit in with an autumn theme and their October-in-New-England wedding.

Their *chuppah* was fashioned from Leslie's father's tallis—simple and traditional—with four poles held aloft by four friends. Other traditions were woven into their wedding. On Shabbat, Leslie's parents hosted a festive meal for out-of-town guests; Mark had an *aufruf* the Shabbat before the wedding. Because it was a long holiday weekend, the Berni family hosted a brunch on Monday for friends and traveling guests.

The glories of the season were reflected everywhere in the rich oranges, reds, rusts and yellows of a northeastern

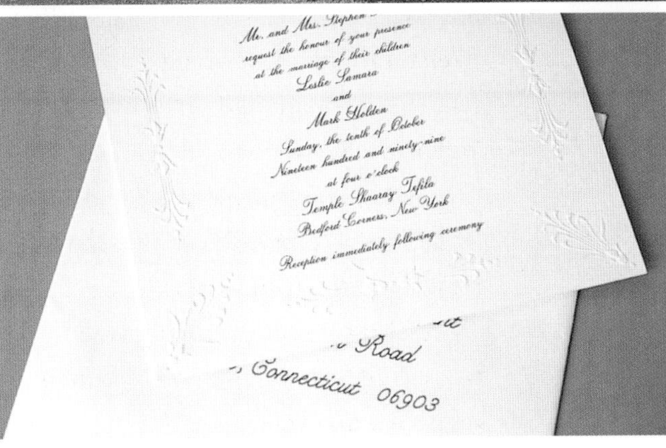

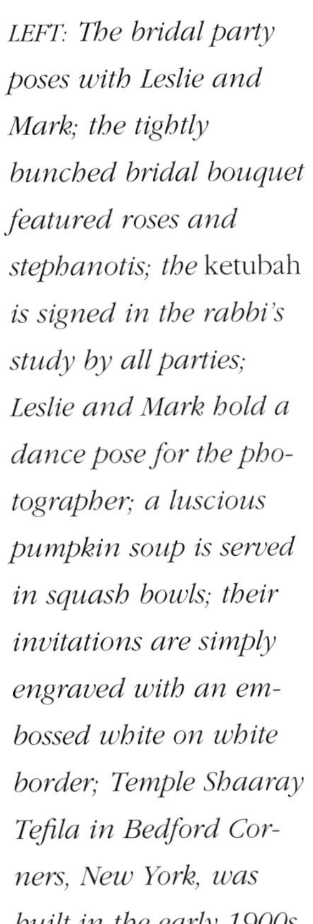

❦ *CLOCKWISE FROM TOP LEFT: The bridal party poses with Leslie and Mark; the tightly bunched bridal bouquet featured roses and stephanotis; the* ketubah *is signed in the rabbi's study by all parties; Leslie and Mark hold a dance pose for the photographer; a luscious pumpkin soup is served in squash bowls; their invitations are simply engraved with an embossed white on white border; Temple Shaaray Tefila in Bedford Corners, New York, was built in the early 1900s.*

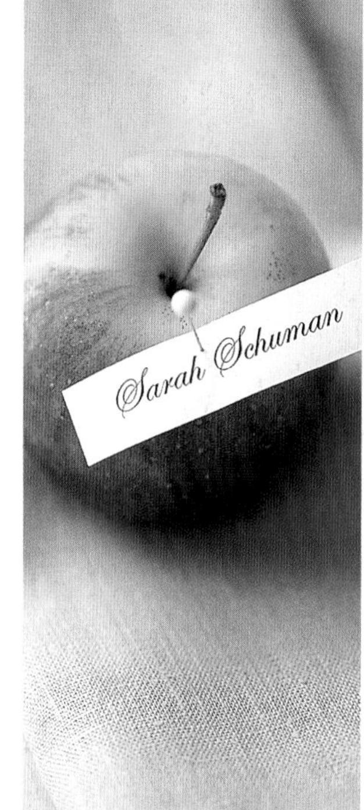

❦ *CLOCKWISE FROM TOP LEFT: Leslie and her dad, Harvey Caney, share a private moment together; tender smiles after the ceremony; wildflower seeds were unique table favors and reflected their love of the outdoors; place-card holders were crunchy regional apples.*

❦ *OPPOSITE PAGE: A lavish spill of fall hydrangea, three kinds of roses—Leonidis, Vendula, and deep red, Hypericum, and seeded eucalyptus brought the season inside, naturally.*

autumn at its peak. Pumpkins and gourds were heaped generously everywhere; hydrangeas and late-blooming Leonidas and Vendula roses made beautiful centerpieces. Guests found packets of wildflower seeds as take-home favors—permanent reminders of this very special wedding. Even the soup was a conversation piece, served in hollowed-out squash bowls.

Leslie and Mark ended up with a wedding true to their own unique style—including their choice of a beautiful rural setting, interwoven with Jewish symbolism and traditions and most important—sealed with their love for each other, born again in the hometown where their friendship first took root.

Let a man be careful to honor his wife, for to her alone belongs the blessings of their home.

Talmud, Baba Metzia 59a

CHAPTER FIVE

AFTER THE wedding

THE WEDDING MAY BE OVER, BUT THE CELEBRATIONS have just begun. For now begins the week of *Sheva Brachas,* the Seven Blessings, an ancient tradition that has been enjoying a respectable comeback in recent years.

The honeymoon is postponed, and the couple are treated to a series of parties and dinners, given by their friends and relatives, in the week following the wedding. Kosher restaurants are booked far in advance on weekday nights for these occasions, and the mood is festive, as scores of well-wishers get together to fete the new couple. Many of these parties are given in various homes as well.

After the honeymoon, the new couple gets down to the business of organizing a Jewish home. This chapter also discusses the concept of a Jewish home, which is considered even more important than the synagogue. The ideal is to approximate the very first Jewish home—that of Sarah and Abraham, where the primary concern of each was the well-being and happiness of the other.

The decision to make your home spiritually richer with mezuzahs on your doorposts or by maintaining a kosher kitchen is an intensely personal one. These decisions should be informed and knowledgeable ones. We introduce some of the practical and spiritual dimensions of these important parts of Jewish life in this chapter.

It's our wish for you that your new home be filled with the same spirit of love and kindliness as was the home of Sarah and Abraham.

the week of *sheva brachas*

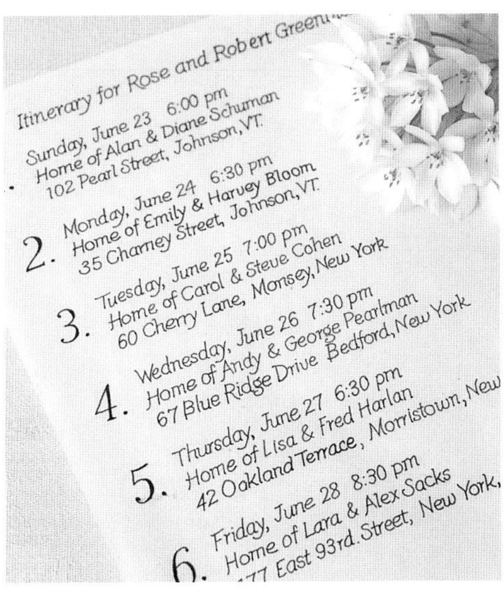

Itinerary for Rose and Robert Green
Sunday, June 23 6:00 pm
Home of Alan & Diane Schuman
102 Pearl Street, Johnson, VT
2. Monday, June 24 6:30 pm
Home of Emily & Harvey Bloom
35 Charney Street, Johnson, VT
3. Tuesday, June 25 7:00 pm
Home of Carol & Steve Cohen
60 Cherry Lane, Monsey, New York
4. Wednesday, June 26 7:30 pm
Home of Andy & George Pearlman
67 Blue Ridge Drive Bedford, New York
5. Thursday, June 27 6:30 pm
Home of Lisa & Fred Harlan
42 Oakland Terrace, Morristown, New
6. Friday, June 28 8:30 pm
Home of Lara & Alex Sacks
East 93rd. Street, New York,

THE SEVEN BLESSINGS. These are recited for the first time under the *chuppah* as part of the actual wedding ceremony. They are repeated again at the end of the wedding meal and now signal the start of a week of celebrations.

This age-old custom has enjoyed a revival in recent years, and the week of parties in the couple's honor is hosted by family or friends. For first marriages, the custom is to have seven separate parties; for second marriages, there are usually three. This custom is based on the biblical telling of Jacob and Leah's weeklong celebration of their marriage. During this week the couple puts aside all business transactions and simply enjoys being together and looking forward to each day's event. *Sheva brachas* can take place in a restaurant or with Chinese takeout at the home of a close friend, or may involve an entire meal, either catered or made at home. All are in celebration of the newly married couple, who postpone their honeymoon trip for a week to attend these celebrations. Each day, it is a special mitzvah to have a *panim chadashot*, or new face, among the guests, to keep the rejoicing fresh.

During the week of *Sheva Brachas,* the bridal couple is treated like royalty and feted for seven nights by friends and relatives, who vie for the opportunity of fulfilling the mitzvah of entertaining the couple. Toasts interrupt the meal during each course, which gives the hosts time to pace themselves and still enjoy the festivities.

The week of the *Sheva Brachas* continues the excitement of the wedding and even has some advantages. The new couple have no decisions to make, and their only responsibility is to show up at the appointed time and place and enjoy themselves. It's a great post-wedding gift, and those involved seem to relish arranging the itinerary and coordinating the guest lists.

❦ *OPPOSITE: A delicate, luscious salmon roll slices into an interesting pinwheel design, creating a visual crowd pleaser.*

Sheva Bracha Dinner Menu

Vegetarian Chopped Liver

Salmon Roll with Dill Sauce

Fresh Asparagus

Sheet Potatoes

Orange Carrot Cake

If you are planning on hosting a *Sheva Brachas* celebration, here is an offering that is sure to enhance the festivities—featuring a luscious salmon roll that's easy to double or triple. It can be prepared a day or so ahead and freshly baked just before the guests arrive. So, if you're having a *Sheva Brachas* party for some special friends (maybe you introduced them!) this is the perfect meal, and one they'll remember.

If you're entertaining at home, make the newlyweds feel even more special by seating them in special chairs. (See page 73 for chair ideas.) Treat them to special wine flutes, too. Just for fun, English "crackers" get the evening off to a bang—they're party favors with pull tabs that make noise and spill fun favors.

Now, for some meal highlights. Our vegetarian chopped liver will fool the most devoted meat-and-potatoes fan. It's creamy, satisfying, and delicious, and best of all, you can prepare it a week ahead. Topped with chopped sweet onions and served on a bed of field greens tossed with balsamic vinegar and a good olive oil, our faux liver is the beginning of a memorable meal.

For dessert, the orange carrot cake is a welcome break from the never-ending parade of chocolate finales that have been served all week. The tang of oranges gives this cake a delicate taste, a wonderful texture, and a moistness that also allows you to bake ahead of time with fabulous results.

At the conclusion of the meal, the Seven Blessings are recited—these are the same blessings recited in the wedding ceremony. They are recited over two cups of wine that are mixed into a third cup. This symbolizes two lives coming together to create one, and both the newlyweds drink from the third cup.

The pleated invitations shown above are fast, easy, and fun to receive. Easy to create on your computer, they fold, accordion-style, to fit into a standard envelope. The design spells out the couple's names, but this is just a suggestion. Get creative with graphics, or wrap and tie the folded paper with natural jute or a silky ribbon before slipping it into envelopes. Again, the heavy, handmade papers with textual interest make a unique statement that only looks outrageously expensive. Standard envelopes come in wonderful, offbeat shades, and you can "seal" each with a square, heart or abstract cutout of leftover handmade papers from the invitations—just use a dab of glue or some spray mount.

❦ *ABOVE: An accordion-folded invitation is made simply on the computer, and folds neatly into a standard envelope.*

❦ *OPPOSITE: Cream cheese frosting is the perfect complement to the moist, luscious flavor of carrot cake, a perennial American favorite.*

❦ *ABOVE: Tie up a take-home memento of the wedding festivities. Thread "framed" wedding candids with silky ribbons for unique napkin rings.*

These *Sheva Brachas* napkin tie-ups are a unique and personal way to honor the new couple, and all you need are some wedding snapshots, scissors, glue, ribbon lengths, and your friendly neighborhood copy center.

The napkin ties shown all feature the same photo, but it might be fun to use as many as a dozen different candid photos of the bride and groom. Here's all you do: Spray mount your photo on one sheet of paper and have color copies made. Just make sure you have one photo for each guest. Cut out the photos, and mount them on heavy colored paper; try the beautiful handmade colored papers at your art supply store. Some are made with pressed flowers and leaves, bits of fiber, lots of texture—even marbleized and metallic looks. After the photos are mounted, punch a hole in the left-hand corner (use a heart-shaped paper punch!), thread through the ribbon, and tie the souvenir photos onto rolled napkins. Stack them in a wooden tray or pretty basket.

Just a reminder—make the photos a size that fits into a small frame to make it easier for guests to have a lasting memory of this happy time. Or, try laminating the photos and affixing a one-inch piece of magnet strip—sold in rolls with self-stick backs—onto the back of each. Perfect as a fridge or office magnet!

VEGETARIAN CHOPPED LIVER

SERVES 6 TO 8

3 onions, sliced
½ cup oil
10 Ritz crackers
10 whole walnuts, shelled
1 (8-ounce) can string beans
1 (8-ounce) can green peas
6 hard-boiled eggs

1. Sauté the onions in the oil until golden. Set aside.
2. In a food processor fitted with the steel "S" blade, process the crackers and walnuts. Add the drained string beans and peas.
3. Add the eggs and sautéd onions until well mixed. Remove to a clean container. Chill for at least 1 hour or up to 3 days.
4. Serve on greens, garnished with herbs.

SALMON ROLL WITH DILL SAUCE

SERVES 6 TO 8

1 salmon filet, about 3½ pounds, skin and small bones removed
2 (10-ounce) boxes frozen leaf spinach, thawed
Juice and zest of 1 lemon
2 teaspoons olive oil
4 cloves garlic, peeled and minced
Salt and pepper to taste

DILL SAUCE
2 tablespoons butter
2 tablespoons flour
1 cup white wine
4 tablespoons chopped fresh dill
Salt and pepper to taste

1. Preheat oven to 375°F.
2. Using a sharp knife, slice the filet horizontally, but not all the way through. Fold top over and lay the filet flat.
3. Between two sheets of plastic wrap, carefully pound the filet to an even thickness. Remove plastic.
4. Drain the spinach and spread over the fish. Press into fish and spoon lemon juice on top.
5. Roll up salmon. Cover roll with foil and chill for 1 hour.
6. Mix olive oil, garlic, lemon zest, salt, and pepper to form a paste.
7. Remove foil from the salmon roll and brush with the paste. Rewrap the roll in a layer of greased foil. Place in roasting pan and bake for 45 minutes.
8. Remove from oven and let stand 20 minutes. Using a sharp knife, slice into 1-inch portions and serve with dill sauce.

To prepare dill sauce:
1. Melt butter in a small saucepan over low heat. Add flour; stir until smooth.
2. Gradually add the wine, stirring often until thick and well blended.
3. Add chopped dill, salt, and pepper.

SHEET POTATOES

SERVES 6 TO 8

3 sticks margarine, melted
12 baking potatoes, peeled and thinly sliced
Salt and pepper to taste
3 tablespoons fresh thyme

1. Preheat oven to 400°F.
2. Brush jelly roll pan with some of the melted margarine. Arrange potato slices in overlapping rows in pan and season with salt and pepper.
3. Pour remaining margarine over all and sprinkle with the thyme. Bake for 45 minutes until potatoes are crisp and golden brown.

ORANGE CARROT CAKE

SERVES 8 TO 12

3 cups flour
2 cups sugar
2½ teaspoons baking soda
2½ teaspoons cinnamon
1 teaspoon salt
2 cups shredded carrots (4 medium)
1¼ cups oil
2 teaspoons vanilla extract
1 teaspoon orange peel
1 (11-ounce) can mandarin oranges, not drained
3 eggs

FROSTING
1 (8-ounce) package cream cheese
2 tablespoons butter, melted
1 teaspoon vanilla
3 cups powdered sugar
Chopped nuts for garnish

1. Preheat oven to 350°F.
2. Grease a 13- by 9-inch baking pan. In a large bowl blend all but the frosting ingredients. Beat 2 minutes.
3. Pour into pan and bake 45 to 55 minutes.
4. Blend all the frosting ingredients until smooth.
5. Frost the cooled cake. Garnish with walnuts.

Friday Night

The most wonderful of all the nights of *Sheva Brachas* week is Friday night, the start of Shabbat.

The evening begins with the lighting of Shabbat candles.

Before the meal is begun, a Kiddush prayer is said over wine and everyone has a sip.

The meal begins with the *motzi* prayer over the challahs and everyone partaking of a slice.

A traditional Friday night meal starts with gefilte fish. Matzoh ball soup, also a Friday night standard, is followed by the main course which is usually chicken. Other offerings often include kugels (potato or noodle) and a variety of salads.

It doesn't really matter if you favor the traditional Friday night meal or prefer vegetarian fare. What's important is to honor Shabbat as well as the newlyweds.

Sara & Evan Dreyfuss
1264 Clayton Dr.
St. Louis, MO. 63146
CyberCubes.com
AMB

a note of thanks

THE WEDDING IS OVER. YOUR PHOTO proofs are in, and you're easing into your new life. Last but not least are the thank-you notes for the lovely pile of gifts, chosen with care and given with love by family and friends. Get started as soon as you can—you'll be finished sooner, and you'll be able to take that final sigh of relief.

You have lots of choices from the stationery stores for thank-you notes, but here we give you some creative, home-made choices.

Everyone loves photos. Create a card with a collage of wedding snaps by ganging a group of color shots and having them run off at the copy center. The staff will help copy, score, and fold them and sell you envelopes to pop them in, as well.

Make a statement with rubber stamps. They come in an astonishing array of types, including leaves, flowers, even romantic themes. Many already have poems or expressions of thanks in beautiful type fonts. If you see a lovely image in a book or magazine, take it to the copy center and they'll make a personalized rubber stamp for you. Don't forget about papers—from thick, handmade papers to those preprinted styles used by scrapbookers, the choice is yours. Take a look at some of our ideas for inspiration and then, get going.

❦ *OPPOSITE: Accordion-style photo mailers are a special way to share wedding memories and express your thanks with a mini wedding album—they're easy to make or you can purchase them from specialty stores. Try a photo cube—these are from a program called Cybercubes and allow you to plug in six photos. Mail them flat—the recipient, by folding, creates a 3-D photo cube. Try framing a photo on a standard die-cut card, then tie up with a bow.*

❦ *ABOVE, FROM LEFT: A simple gray card with silver trim has slits with the couple's names inserted for a personalized, classic look; rubber stamps from the toy store go luxe using silver ink for stamping; the* todah rabah *expresses thanks in Hebrew; in English, thank-you stamps have an added dash of color with inks, papers, and ribbons.*

memories to display

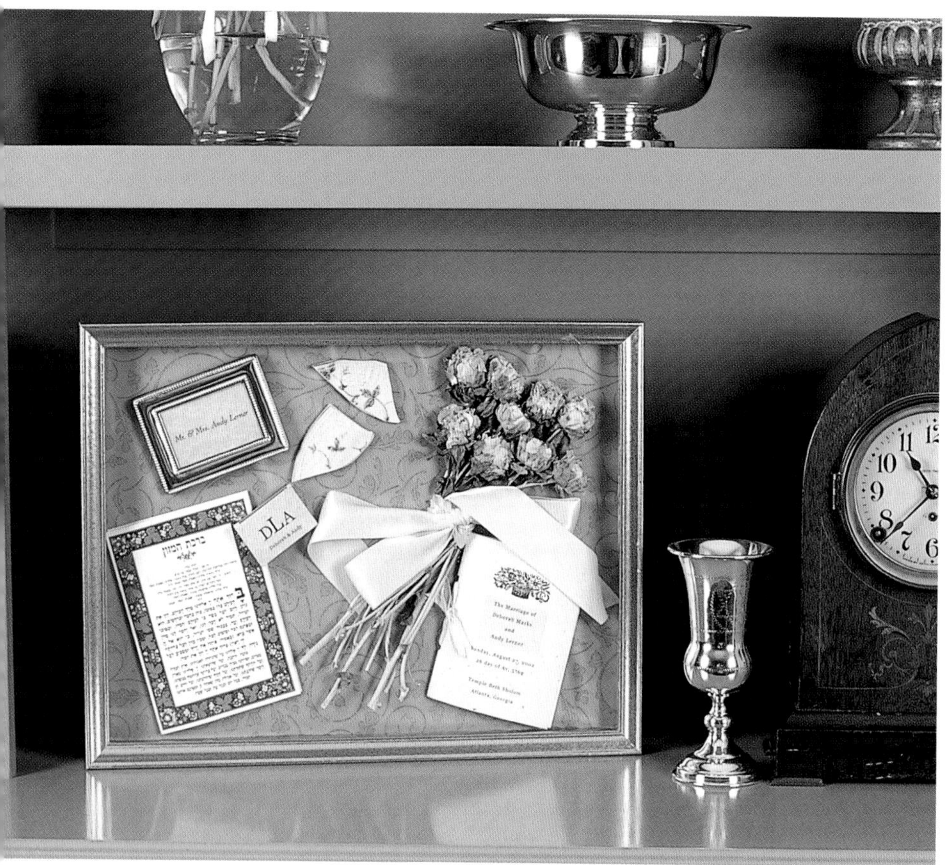

❦ *ABOVE: A shadow box is a good way to display wedding keepsakes.*

❦ *OPPOSITE: A* ketubah *by artist Mickie Caspi is beautifully framed in gold.*

SETTING UP YOUR NEW HOME together is an exciting time. Bring some of the excitement and spirit of your wedding into the fabric of your everyday lives—to admire, to remember, and to make *shalom bayit* (a happy home) a permanent presence.

Many couples hang their *ketubah* over their bed; others place it near the entryway of their homes as a sort of greeting to those who enter.

Since your *Ketubah* was chosen not just for its written content but for its design elements as well, make sure you frame it. Have your *ketubah* mounted on acid-free paper so that it can become an heirloom, and have it framed with non-glare glass. Because your first home probably won't be your last over the years, choose a classic frame that will withstand the test of time and taste—always better underdone than over. Soft, antiqued silvers and golds are good choices, and so are rich woods, perhaps with a small bead or egg-and-dart border pattern. The frame should never compete with the artwork.

Consider a shadow box to hold some treasured wedding memories. The box on the left contains a piece of the broken plate from the engagement party, the wedding program, a matchbook with the couple's names and wedding date, a name card, a Hebrew *bencher,* and the bride's dried bouquet. Get these shadow box frames in lots of wood finishes at large craft chains, or you may go to a custom framer with the components, choose a frame, and an expert will help you assemble it to your specifications.

Whatever memories you decide to incorporate into your home décor, choose your favorites with care and display them with love.

I am my beloved's
אני לדודי ודודי לי
my beloved is mine

mezuzahs

CONTRARY TO POPULAR BELIEF, A mezuzah is not a good luck charm. The purpose of having a mezuzah in one's home is a reminder to love and worship God. The Hebrew word *mezuzah* literally means "doorpost" and is also used to refer to the parchment inside the mezuzah case. The parchment contains two biblical passages: "Hear O Israel, the Lord is our God the Lord is One. . . " (Deut. 6:4–9) and "And if you will carefully obey My commandments . . ." (Deut. 11:13–21). The parchment scroll is rolled up and enclosed in a case.

The mezuzah is affixed to the doorpost on the right side as you enter the home, and there should also be mezuzahs on interior doors as well.

You don't have to be a rabbi to affix a mezuzah. All you need to do is say the following prayer before affixing the mezuzah: *Baruch ata adonai elohainu melech ha-olam asher kidshanu b'mitzvotav v'tzizanu likboa mezuzah.* "Blessed are you Lord our God King of the universe who has commanded us to affix mezuzah."

Jews have always considered the mezuzah to be the ultimate insurance policy. Bringing God's blessings for peace, health, and happiness to everyone in the home. But just as an insurance policy only provides the right coverage if it is written correctly, so too a mezuzah must be "kosher" to be effective. First the mezuzah must be handwritten by a scribe who concentrates on the sacredness of what he is doing the entire time he is writing it. Each letter must be made perfectly. Mezuzahs must be checked every few years because if any of the letters have faded, the mezuzah may no longer be valid. Unfortunately, many of the mezuzahs sold today do not meet the above requirements.

Mezuzah cases can be beautiful and decorative works of art, made of clay, porcelain, wood, metals, or plastic. The variety of cases is endless—from the whimsical for children's rooms to clear cases containing fragments of the wine glass crushed under the *chuppah.*

You can find many lovely mezuzah cases in your local synagogue or Judaica store, or you can make your own. Fimo clay is easy to work with and bakes in a regular oven to harden. It comes in a score of beautiful colors so you can make a case to match your decor.

But whatever the case, the importance of the mezuzah cannot be overstated. Placed at the entrances to all rooms of our home it's a constant reminder that God's presence is everywhere.

❦ *OPPOSITE: Although the mezuzah refers to the parchment inside, the cases come in a rainbow of beautiful choices.*

Mezuzah Tips

If a house has more than one entrance, even if only one is regularly used for coming and going, a mezuzah must be attached at each entrance.

❦

It is suggested that a mezuzah be at the entrance to each of the interior rooms of a home.

❦

It should not be affixed to such rooms as bathrooms.

❦

The mezuzah should be nailed, screwed, or glued to the right side of the door. It is placed at the beginning of the upper third of the doorpost, (at eye level) and tilted at an angle with the upper part slanted inward toward the room and the lower part away from the house.

❦

Have the mezuzah scrolls checked by a rabbi every three or four years.

a kosher kitchen

❦ *ABOVE: The best thing to happen to kosher kitchens are little, peel-off stickers that say "Meat," "Dairy," or "Pareve."*

❦ *OPPOSITE: Bin drawer pulls with a space for inserting a label make perfect sense in a kosher kitchen.*

IF A JEWISH HOME IS A MINIATURE sanctuary, then its table is like an altar. And the kitchen takes on new meaning when it is a kosher kitchen.

However, for many of us, the laws of kashrut may appear obsolete—a throwback to ancient times when certain health precautions were needed that today are no longer necessary.

Kosher foods in many cases *do* have hygienic benefits, but the ultimate benefits are spiritual. Kosher food not only sustains the body, it also nourishes the soul. For thousands of years the very existence of the soul was a topic for debate. But in recent years the emphasis has been more on the relationship of body and soul. The laws of kashrut guide us in bringing the physical and the spiritual, the body and the soul into harmony.

The basic principle of kashrut is the separation of meat and dairy products. The kosher kitchen contains separate sets of dishes, utensils, and cookware, and separate preparation areas for meat and dairy. A third category, parve, is foods that are neither meat nor dairy and may be eaten with either one.

Kosher beef and fowl come only from animals that are neither predators nor scavengers. Each animal is slaughtered individually by a *shochet,* a person skilled in kosher slaughtering. He uses a knife sharpened hundreds of times to ensure the most humane slaughtering possible. He also looks for signs of disease.

If you are planning on having a kosher kitchen, you might want two different color schemes to visually color-code the difference between meat and dairy quickly and efficiently. As for pareve, we always suggest white utensils and pots. You don't need pareve dishes or flatware since pareve foods may be eaten with either meat or dairy dishes.

The mitzvah of kashrut is a treasured tradition that more and more couples at all levels of observance are beginning to adopt. Pass it down to the next generation, with love.

DAIRY
MEAT

glossary of jewish terms

aishes chayil A woman of valor

Ashkenazi Pertaining to Jews of Central, Eastern, and Western European descent

aufruf The calling up of the groom to recite the blessings over the Torah on the Shabbat before the wedding

badeken The placing of the veil over the bride done by the groom prior to the wedding ceremony

barshert Meant to be; intended one

bencher A grace-after-meal booklet

berberisca Spanish word meaning "henna night"; the ceremony that takes place several days before a Sephardic wedding

betrothal The first part of the wedding ceremony, consisting of the preliminary benediction, the proposal, and the giving of the ring—in Hebrew, *kiddushin*

bimah The platform in the synagogue from which the rabbi or cantor conducts the services

challah The traditional braided bread served on the Shabbat, holidays, and joyous occasions.

chavurah A nonformal gathering of friends and family for services, etc.

chazen A cantor

chesed kindness

chosen tish The groom's table, signifying the reception he is accorded just prior to the *chuppah*

chuppah The bridal canopy; also a legal term for the final part of the marriage ceremony

erusin The formal betrothal of the bride and groom constituting the first part of the wedding ceremony

hakhnasal kallah Funds for poor brides

Halacha Jewish law

hamsa A Sephardic charm in the shape of a hand, said to be good luck

Hasidim: Jews who go beyond the letter of the law, followers of the Hasidic movement

Havdalah candle A multiwicked candle, usually braided, that is lit at the end of the Shabbat

hiddur mitzvah The beautifying of a mitzvah

horah Traditional Jewish folk dance, performed in a circle

Kabbalah: The deep inner dimensions of the Torah

kabbalat panim Prenuptial reception; held separately by the bride and groom

Kaddish: Mourner's prayer

kashrut To follow the laws of keeping kosher

keswa el kbira The lavish outfit worn by Sephardic brides on the henna night

ketubah The marriage contract

Kiddush The blessing said over wine to sanctify the beginning of Shabbat or a holiday

kiddushin Sanctity; also used as a synonym for "marriage"

kinyan A legal term denoting the process of acquisition

kiskallah A special chair for the bride to sit on while she receives good wishes from guests before the wedding

kittle A white garment worn on holidays and also by grooms at their weddings

klezmer A Yiddish word referring to music that originated in the shtetels of Eastern Europe before World War II

kosher Any food that is fit, proper, or in accordance with Jewish law

L'Chaim "To life"—a toast

Lubavitch A sect of Hasidic Jews known for their efforts to promote the observance of Judaism among other Jews

mayim hayyim "Living waters"; water that comes from a natural source

mazel tov Congratulations; "good luck"

mezuzah A handwritten scroll, on which are written two biblical passages, that are affixed to the doorposts of Jewish homes

Midrash A critical interpretation of scripture often containing a moral lesson

mikvah A ritual pool used for purposes of purification

minyan A quorum of ten adult males required for public religious worship

mitzvah An obligation of the Jewish faith; meaning "to bind" to God

motzi Blessing said over bread

nesuin Nuptials

panim chadashot "New face" that is required at the seven *Sheva Brachas* celebrations the first week of marriage

pareve Food with ingredients of neither dairy nor animal origin

perutah An ancient coin

rebbe A mentor or teacher for his followers

ruach Joyous; literally "spirit"

Sephardim Jews of Spanish origin who come from Africa, the Middle East, southern Europe, and Asia

Shabbat The Sabbath

shadkhan A matchmaker

shalom bayit Peace in the home

shtetels The small Jewish towns and villages of pre-World War II Europe

Sheva Brachas The Seven Blessings said first during the wedding ceremony and then in the grace after meals; also refers to the week of festive meals following the wedding

shiddach The matching of a man and woman for the purpose of marriage

shluchim Messengers or envoys

shochet A ritual slaughterer

simcha A joyous occasion

tallis Prayer shawl

Talmud The oral teachings of the Torah, including the Mishna and the Gemora

tansel The symbolic dance at Hasidic weddings between the rabbi and bride

Tay-Sachs A genetic disease affecting one in every 2,500 Ashkenazi Jewish newborns

tenaim A formal engagement contract

todah rabah Hebrew for "thank you very much"

Torah The five books of Moses; the Bible

***tzedakah* box** A charity box.

tzinus The practice of being modest in dress, appearance, and behavior

yarmulkah A ritual head covering

yeshiva A school of Jewish learning

yichud Literally "together"; brief seclusion of bride and groom immediately following the wedding ceremony

Yom Kippur Day of Atonement.

resource guide

PAGE 2
Wedding rings, courtesy of the Judaica Store, West Hartford, CT, 860-236-9956

PAGE 20
Cake toppers, from the private collection of Ellen Roth.

PAGE 35
Olive green bowl, Pottery Barn, 1-888-770-5176, www.potterybarn.com

PAGE 37
Papers and ribbon, Michael's Crafts, 1-800-MICHAELS (1-800-642-4235), www.michaels.com

PAGE 38
Glass cake stands, Williams-Sonoma, 1-800-541-2233
Silver cookie stand, Pottery Barn, 1-888-770-5176

PAGE 41
Wissotsky tea sampler, The Source for Everything Jewish, 1-800-426-2567, www.jewishsource.com
Havdalah candles, Aunt Sadie's Candlestix, www.sweetpeashome.com
Edible crystallized flowers, Meadowsweets, 1-888-827-6477, www.candiedflowers.com
Pastries, Audra Weisel

Ketubahs
Many of the artists featured in this book can be found at
e.ketubah.com;
Ketubah/Ketubah
1-888-KETUBAH (1-888-538-8224)
www.ketubah.com;
The Ketubah Collection, 1-888-920-3636, www.ketubahcollection.com;
The Ketubah Gallery,
1-888-884-3004,
www.ketubah-gallery.com

PAGE 44
"Gates" *ketubah,* by Jonathan Kremer, 1-610-664-9625, www.kremerdesigns.com

PAGE 45
Cut-paper *ketubah,* by Ardyn Halter in Israel, 06-6373508, ardynket@netvision.net.il

PAGE 46
"The Four Seasons" Ketubah, by Naomi Teplow, www.ketubotbynaomi..com
"Double Ring" *ketubah,* by Jeanette Kuvin Oren, 1-203-389-6077, www.KuvinOren.com

PAGE 47
"Jerusalem Garden" *ketubah,* by Ardyn Halter in Israel, 06-6373508, ardynket@netvision.net.il
"Emanu-El" *ketubah,* by Micah Parker Artworks, 1-888-33-MICAH (1-888-336-4224), www.micahparkerartworks.com

PAGE 48
Floral *ketubah,* by Laya Crust, 1-416-635-7356, llight@interlog.com
Acqui *ketubah,* by William Newman, Calligraphics, 1-800-354-4550, calligrfx@aol.com

PAGE 49
"The Tree of Life" *ketubah,* by Howard Fox, Ketubah/Ketubah, 1-888-KETUBAH (1-888-538-8224), www.ketubah.com
Arch *ketubah,* by Bobbi Yoffee, 1-904-733-9619, scribemom@attbi.com
"Tapestry" *ketubah,* by Jonathan Kremer, 1-610-664-9625, www.kremerdesigns.com

Invitations
Most invitations below are sold in high-end retail establishments, nationwide.

PAGE 51
All invitations except for bottom left: Checkerboard Limited, 1-800-735-2475, info@checkernet.com, www.eInvite.com
Bottom left invitation: Regency, 1-800-847-5055

PAGE 52
Invitations, Paper Direct, 1-800-272-7377, www.paperdirect.com

PAGE 53
Invitations, *Top and top right:* Fitzgraphics, Inc., 1-800-662-8200, www.fitzgraphics.com
Center and bottom right: William Arthur, 1-800-985-6581, www.williamarthur.com
Bottom left: Julie Holcomb Printers, 1-510-654-6416, www.julieholcombprinters.com

Other letterpress printers:
Robin Price, 1-860-344-8644, rprice@wesleyan.edu
Mission Creek Press, 1-866-MCPRESS (1-866-627-7377), www.missioncreekpress.com

PAGE 65
Adirondack *chuppah*, Adirondack Rustic studio, Dee Carnelli, artist/owner, 1-860-489-6767
Location: The Rose Garden, Elizabeth Park, Hartford, CT

PAGE 69
Velvet *chuppah*, Velvet and tassels from Jo-Ann Fabric & Crafts, www.joann.com
Location: Charter Oak Cultural Center, Hartford, CT

PAGE 72
Painted chairs, designed by Daniella Zandsberg, painted by the students of Yachad Hebrew High School, West Hartford, CT.
Also, artist Jeanette Kuvin Oren custom-paints "Simcha Chairs," 1-203-389-6077, www.simchachairs.com
Location: The Simsbury Inn, Simsbury, CT, 1-860-392-0314, www.simsburyinn.com

PAGE 77
Programs, Skeletal leaves, Michael's Crafts, 1-800-MICHAELS (1-800-642-4235), www.michaels.com
Initial stencil, Delta Stencil Magic, Whittier, CA, www.deltacrafts.com

PAGE 78
Yarmulkahs, 1-800-KIPPOTT (1-547-7688), www.kipot.com
Organza sheer bags, www.bag-its.com
Colored, patterned papers, Michael's Crafts, 1-800-MICHAELS (1-800-642-4235), www.michaels.com
Clear acetate name cards, Staples copy department; ask for copies on clear acetate overhead stock. Check www.staples.com for a location near you.

PAGE 83
CD, www.imix.com, approximately $11 per CD of five songs.
Initial stickers, Martha By Mail, 1-800-950-7130, www.marthastewart.com
White boxes, Paper Mart, 1-800-745-8800, www.papermart.com
Initial lollipops, Alphabet Delights, 1-800-377-4368, Kencraft, 119 E. 200 N. Alpine, UT 84004

PAGE 84
Organza favor bags, www.bag-its.com
Glass cylinders, AC Moore
Glass frame, Target, 1-800-304-4000, www.target.com
Location: The Simsbury Inn, Simsbury, CT, 1-860-392-0314, www.simsburyinn.com

PAGE 89
White urn, Michael's Crafts, 1-800-MICHAELS (1-800-642-4235), www.michaels.com
Tablecloth, Williams-Sonoma, 1-800-541-2233

PAGE 93
Metal baskets and vellum gift bags, Michael's Crafts, 1-800-MICHAELS (1-800-642-4235), www.michaels.com

Mini shopping cart, Target, 1-800-304-4000, www.target.com

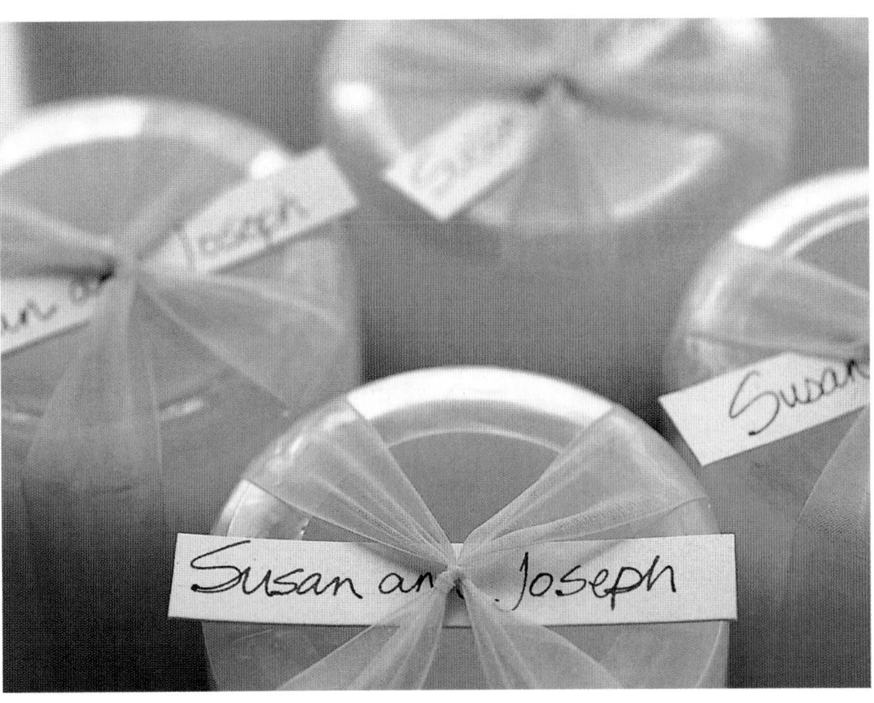

PAGE 99
Wedding Day Mitzvahs
This organization has raised money for over five hundred weddings for those less fortunate:

Keren Simchat Chassan V'Kallah, 706 Montgomery Street, Brooklyn, NY 11213; contact Devorah Benjamin by e-mail: kallah5760@aol.com

The following organizations will lend your wedding gown, veil, and mother's and/or bridesmaid's gowns to those less fortunate:

Eretz Tova Bridal Fund, 18 Heyward Street, Brooklyn, NY 11211, 1-718-243-2495

N'shei Ahavas Chesed, c/o Women's League for Community Services, 1680 47th Street, Brooklyn, NY 11204; contact Blimi Blustein, 1-212-851-1812

Daniel Kuttler Charity Fund, Karen Hayesod Street 7, Jerusalem, Israel,

Rabbanit Bracha Kapach, 12 Lod Street, Jerusalem, Israel

The following Web sites can offer links to local food banks that will pick up the leftover food from your reception site and take it to a homeless shelter, soup kitchen, or food pantry:

candlelightstories.com, secondharvest.org

PAGES 104
Robyn Finklestein and Jared Fischer
Flowers, Petals, 1-516-674-9325
Catering, The University Club
Band, Doug Winters, 1-914-238-9100 Best Kept Secret

PAGES 116–121
Jacqueline Sherman and Bennett Gross
Flowers, Paul Kaufman, Kauffman's Studio Flora, 1-800-601-9226
Catering, The Four Seasons Aviara
Band, Sean Holt Band, It's the Main Event/Bob Gail Productions, 1-310-276-3300

PAGES 128–133
Esther Ehrman and Andrew Sirotnik
Flowers, Fleurish, 1-206-322-1602
Catering, Theodora van den Beld, The Yakima Grill, 1-206-956-0639

PAGES 134–139
Lori Weitzman and Michael Bernstein
Party planner, Bruce Sutka, Sutka Productions International, Inc., 1-561-835-8455; **Band,** Manhattan Music, Howard Stuart 1-954-561-5615 **Flowers and catering,** The Mar-A-Lago Club; **Videographer,** Lighting Videos, John Koterba, 1-561-641-8181.

PAGES 140–145
Leslie Caney and Mark Berni
Caterer, Foremost, 1-201-664-2465, **Flowers,** Peter Rodgers, 1-203-327-4170; **Reception,** Shaaray Tefila, 1-914-666-3133

PAGES 148
Dinner plate, Bed Bath and Beyond, 1-800-GO BEYOND (1-800-462-3966), www.bedbathandbeyond.com

PAGES 150
Dessert plate, Laura Ashley, www.lauraashley.com

PAGES 154
Accordion mailer, Kolo, LLC, www.kolo-usa.com; **Photo cube,** Cybercubes, www.CyberCubes.com, **Photo card,** Jam Paper & Envelope, 1-800-8010-JAM, www.jampaper.com

PAGES 155
Name rubber stamps, Inkadinkado, www.inkadinkado.com, **Thank-you rubber stamp,** All Night Media, Inc., www.allnightmedia.com

PAGES 156
Shadow box, Michael's Crafts 1-800-MICHAELS (1-800-642-4235), www.michaels.com or www.mymemorybox.com

PAGES 157
Ketubah, by Micki Caspi, www.ajp.com/shop/caspi.html

photographers

Principal Photographer

Shaffer/Smith Photography
Dawn Smith, Jeff Shaffer
New York, NY
1-212-982-9620
www.shaffersmith.com

Wedding Photographers

Paul Barnett
San Diego, CA
1-619-285-1207
www.barnettphoto.com

Debranne & Company
Connecticut, Nantucket, New York
1-203-254-7734
1-877-452-3686 (toll free)
www.debranne.com

Cre8me Inc.
Leo Reinfeld
Venezuela, Miami, FL
1-954-923-1941
www.cre8me.com

Davidoff Studios
Babe Davidoff
Palm Beach, FL
1-561-655-1164

Janet Klinger Photography
Seattle, WA
1-206-622-7478
www.janetklinger.com

Jasper/Sky Photography
Stephanie Jasper, Paul Sky
Worldwide
1-800-357-8011

Mendel Meyers Studios
Brooklyn, NY
1-718-438-3744

André Maier
New York, NY
1-212-388-2272
www.andremaier.com

Fred Marcus Photography
Andy Marcus
New York, NY
1-212-873-5588
www.fredmarcus.com

Visions in Photography
Robert E. Acevedo
Rockville, MD
1-301-279-0538

references

Brayer, Menachem. *The Jewish Woman in Rabbinic Literature.* Hoboken, NJ: Ktav Publishing House, Inc., 1986.

Feldman, Emanuel. *One Plus One Equals One.* Jerusalem: Feldheim Publishers, 1999.

Goodman, Philip, and Hanna Goodman. *The Jewish Marriage Anthology.* Philadelphia, PA: Jewish Publication Society of America, 1965.

Isaacs, Rabbi Ronald H. *The Bride and Groom Handbook.* West Orange, NJ: Behrman House, Inc., 1987.

Kaplan, Rabbi Aryeh. *Made in Heaven: A Jewish Wedding Guide.* Brooklyn, NY: Moznaim Publishing Corp., 1983.

Kaufman, Michael. *Love, Marriage and Family in Jewish Law and Tradition.* Northvale, NJ: Jason Aronson Inc., 1992.

Lamm, Maurice. *The Jewish Way in Love and Marriage.* San Francisco: Harper & Row, 1980.

credits

Robert E. Acevedo: 68

Paul Barnett: 58, 75, 86 (*top*), 117–19 (*top right, center left and right*), 120–121

Debranne Cingari: 140, 142, 143 (*top right and left, center right and left*), 144 (*top left and right*)

Cre8me Inc: 111, 112 (*top left, center right*), 113, 114 (*top right, center left, bottom*)

Davidoff Studios: 134–35, 136 (*top left, top right, and bottom*), 137, 138 (*top, bottom center*), 139

Janet Klinger: 128, 129, 130–33

Jasper/Sky: 87, 88

The Jewish Historical Society of Greater Hartford: 19

The Jewish Museum, NY/Art Resource, NY: 16, 18 (*top row center, middle row right*), 21 (*top*)

Erich Lessing/Art Resource, NY: 21 (*bottom*)

Mendel Meyers: 122–24, 125 (*top left, top and bottom right*), 126 (*bottom*), 127

André Maier: 12, 57 (*top*), 67, 103

Fred Marcus Photography: 9, 99, 102, 104–7, 108 (*top right, bottom left and right*), 109 (*top left, bottom left and right*)

Réunion des Musées Nationaux/Art Resource: 18 (*top right, middle left, bottom left and right*)

Shaffer/Smith: 1, 2–3, 5–6, 7 (*top right*), 8, 10, 13, 17, 20, 31–32, 35,

36, 37, 38, 41–42, 44–45, 47–48, 49 (*top, bottom right*), 51–53, 57 (*bottom*), 59–61, 65–66, 69, 71–74, 76–84, 86 (*bottom*), 89–93, 95–98, 108 (*top left, bottom center*), 109 (*top right*), 110, 112 (*top right, center left, bottom*), 114 (*top left, center right*), 115–16, 119 (*top left, bottom right*), 125 (*top center*), 126 (*top*), 136 (*center right*), 138 (*bottom left and right*), 141, 143 (*bottom left and right*), 144 (*center left, bottom right*), 145, 148–52, 154–58, 160–61

Victoria & Albert Museum, NY/Art Resource, NY: 18 (*top left; middle center; bottom center*)

Page 23: (*top*) from the collection of Beth and Donald Salzberg, (*middle*) from the collection of Bobbi and Bob Markowitz, (*bottom*) from the collection of Sarah Jane Freymann and Steven Schwartz
Page 24: from the collection of Rita and Michael Brownstein
Page 25: (*top*) from the collection of Judy and Jeffrey Pardo, (*bottom*) from the collection of Margit and Howard Milos
Page 43: from the collection of Emily Caney

ILLUSTRATIONS
Susan Blubaugh: 62–63

FOOD STYLING
Marie Piraino: 32, 35, 109 (*top right*), 112 (*top right*), 143 (*bottom right*), 148, 150

CAKES
Audra Weisel: 38, 41, 95, 96, 97.

acknowledgments

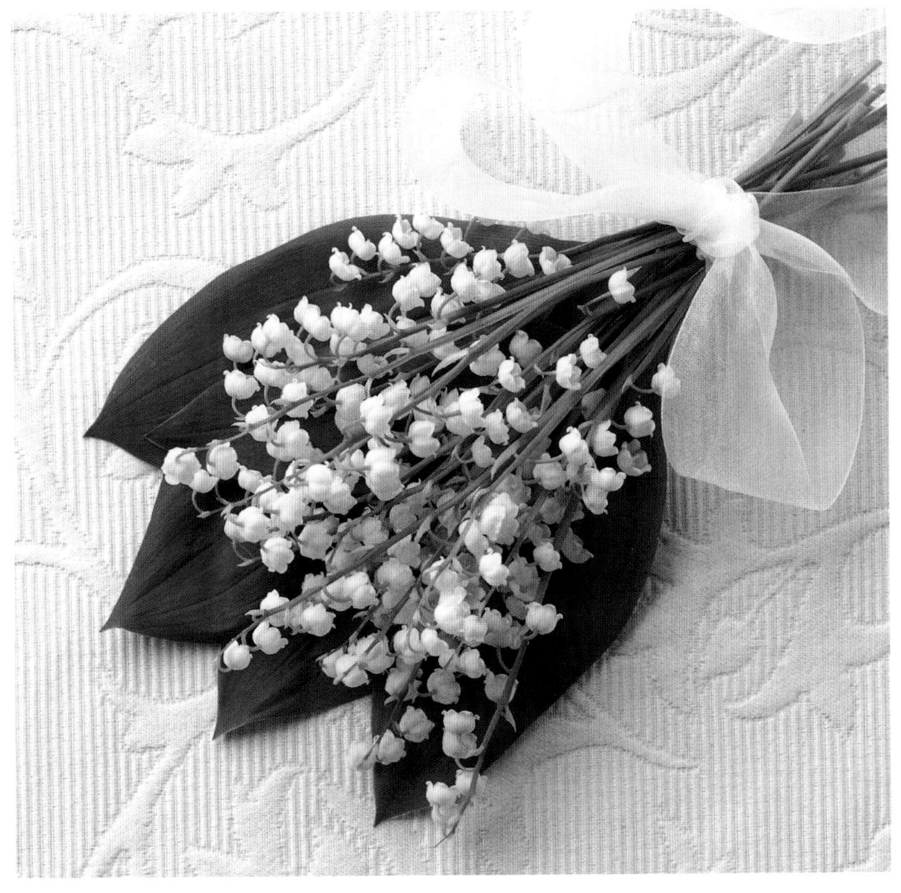

To all the wonderful and talented people who helped make this book possible—thank you.

To my agent, Sarah Jane Freymann, who first suggested the idea of a Jewish wedding book—you are always right!

To my editor at Simon & Schuster, Sydny Miner, and the rest of the marvelous team at Simon & Schuster.

To Dawn Smith, for her meticulous technical and artistic talents and the beautiful photographs they create.

To Donna Wolf Koplowitz: my regard for your writing is matched only by my regard for your friendship.

To Marie Piraino, for the wonderful food styling and to Audra Weisel, for the gorgeous cakes and pastries.

To Ellen Roth, for lending me her collection of cake toppers to be photographed for this book.

To Joseph Boehm, of *Better Homes and Gardens,* for his expert styling advice.

To Susan Blubaugh (my roommate from art school), whose illustrations are always crystal clear and beautiful at the same time.

To the following models: Ilana Kafer, Elizabeth Pomerantz, and Beth Salzberg.

To the Jewish bridal shower participants: Bara Colodne, Alison Kamenetsky, Loni Tackel, Jen Schlosberg, and Melanie Shain.

To the wedding couples—Robyn and Jared Fischer, Dana and Jacob Tangir, Jackie and Bennett Gross, Chana and Shalom Lew, Esther and Andrew Sirotnik, Lori and Michael Bernstein, and Leslie and Mark Berni—for letting me be a part of your weddings and sharing them with our readers.

To Sherri Pliskin, for lending me her beautiful Judaica to be photographed.

For Marsha and Bruce Komarow, Beth and Don Salzberg, and Estelle and Shelton Kafer for allowing me to photograph in their homes.

To the Simsbury Inn, in Simsbury, Connecticut, for allowing me to photograph in their beautiful facility.

To the Charter Oak Cultural Center in Hartford, Connecticut, for allowing me to photograph in the sanctuary.

To Rabbi Mendel Samuels and Rabbi Shlomo Yaffe, who ensured that this book was in accordance with Jewish law.

To my husband, Michael, who refers to my book as "our book"—this is as much his as mine because of all the research and writing he has done.

To the women in my family who never tire of promoting my books to everyone they come across—my mother, Margit Milos; sister Lisa Milos Harlan; sister-in-law Carol Cohen; niece Lara Cohen; and mother-in-law, Lea Brownstein.

index

D

E

After more than a year of eating at the same Chinese restaurant Jackie finally got a fortune
Sherman and Bennett Gross will be married on
OCTOBER 31,
California and more information will be coming shortly on hotels
weekend. We are looking forward to celebrating with you!
Save the date!
Jackie + Bennett
You or a close friend will be married within a year.

HSTEW 296
.444
B885